The Wisdom of V

T0009411

"Transformation has a sound, and it's the voice of Ren Hurst weaving words of wisdom back into the wild flute of our collective spine. Through gorgeous storytelling, Ren explores the devastation of domestication through rewilding experiences with animals. *The Wisdom of Wildness* reanimates deep inner passion for freedom, creation, and the embodied miracle of undomesticated life. This book is an invitation to feel it all AND cultivate lives of sanctuary!"

~ **Amy Tuttle**, wilderness and threshold guide,
council facilitator, and arts and healing practitioner

"A brave and inspiring story that urges us to reclaim the innate wildness within. Ren's 13 principles reflect her dedication to unconditional love and are a foundation for a new, wild, and true relationship not just with the animals we care for but with our authentic animal human selves."

~ **Fay Johnstone**, shamanic herbalist, Reiki teacher, and author of
Plant Spirit Reiki and *Plants That Speak, Souls That Sing*

"*The Wisdom of Wildness* is a brilliant journey of self-discovery. The magic in applying Sanctuary13 principles takes one deeper than imagined to be the conduit of light for oneself while interacting with all of creation, particularly being a conscious human walking the earth. Ren has an uncanny ability to invite the reader into their own infinite and innate wisdom if they are willing to embrace not only the divinity of who they are but the humanness as well. The magical words within this book will invite you to that place of what true self-love is."

~ **Franny Harcey**, HTCP, Healing Touch certified
practitioner and intuitive

"Who do we really want to be in this precious lifetime? Wanting is the first step; getting there amid the many pressures of modern life also takes know-how. Through her many years of experience and experiment to reveal what gets in the way of her own relationships with humans and animals, Ren is now able to offer us a pathway of 13 principles of intention and attention as an essential guide for transformation—what has been for her can now be available for each person willing to commit to such a journey of connection—a connection with oneself and with one another. *The Wisdom of Wildness* is an invitation to embark on a journey inward. For this life quest, these pages become a manual of guidance, as an elder companion would—being there alongside to help prepare, inspire, and support the call to journey deeper than before. Let these become your 13 agreements toward a life well lived. And in so doing, your life as a human being on this earth will meet your soul's birthright."

> ~ **Krystyna Jurzykowski**, council carrier, wilderness guide, cofounder of Fossil Rim Wildlife Center, and owner of High Hope Sanctuary for Retreat

"Ren Hurst has to be one of the most influential and visionary humans I've had the pleasure of encountering. Our conversations have continued to blow my crown chakra right open—and anyone who reads her books are bound to have their belief systems rattled in the most beautiful way. Ren delicately walks our egos through a complete transformation with her ideas on domestication, and those seeking to walk a path toward enlightenment will surely find that within her words."

> ~ **Brittany Quagan**, M.S., LPC, licensed professional counselor and spiritual healer

THE WISDOM OF WILDNESS

HEALING THE TRAUMA OF DOMESTICATION

REN HURST

FINDHORN PRESS

Findhorn Press
One Park Street
Rochester, Vermont 05767
www.findhornpress.com

Text stock is SFI certified

Findhorn Press is a division of Inner Traditions International

Copyright © 2022 by Ren Hurst

All rights reserved. No part of this book may be reproduced or utilized in any form or by any means, electronic or mechanical, including photocopying, recording, or by any information storage and retrieval system, without permission in writing from the publisher.

Disclaimer

The information in this book is given in good faith and intended for information only. Neither author nor publisher can be held liable by any person for any loss or damage whatsoever which may arise from the use of this book or any of the information therein.

Cataloging-in-Publication data for this title is available from the Library of Congress

ISBN 978-1-64411-679-1 (print)
ISBN 978-1-64411-680-7 (ebook)

Printed and bound in the United States by Lake Book Manufacturing, LLC
The text stock is SFI certified. The Sustainable Forestry Initiative® program promotes sustainable forest management.

10 9 8 7 6 5 4 3 2 1

Edited by Nicky Leach
Text design and layout by Richard Crookes
This book was typeset in Adobe Garamond Pro and Gill Sans

To send correspondence to the author of this book, mail a first-class letter to the author c/o Inner Traditions • Bear & Company, One Park Street, Rochester, VT 05767, USA and we will forward the communication, or contact the author directly at **www.rendermewild.com**.

•

For my dearest Spur,

and for all the animals who have sacrificed their lives

or their freedom because we did not know

how to love ourselves.

•

And still, for Annie.

If my love for you were any more common,

books like this need not be written.

•

CONTENTS

＊＊＊＊

If we are fortunate enough to see a White Spirit Animal, it changes us as people.

Because they stand out, we pay more attention to them than their kin. All of the White Spirit Animals teach humanity about the species they are members of—and this explains, in part, why they are all mythologized and revered by the human cultures surrounding them. Simply put, White Spirit Animals are rare yet they represent millions of animals among them.

Each White Spirit Animal is important to the Earth's well-being and, while precious to indigenous cultures dating back thousands of years, they are all endangered species, but also part of prophetic teachings about these emergent times.

- White Spirit Animals by
J. Zohara Meyerhoff Hieronimus, D.H.L.

＊＊＊＊

FOREWORD

The terms "rewild" and "undomesticated" have made their way, rightly so, into our modern-day vernacular as we reach toward a more original integrity of humanness and relationship, with ourselves, each other, and all life on our planet. Our truest selves will never cease this reach, both personal and collective, toward that which we know to be inherently true—which is that no one is free until all are free, and that the true nature of love seeks to serve that emancipation in ways that might surprise us, asking us always to question that which we have taken to be accepted patterns of engagement, perception, and reality, *and to move from the most whole place within.*

Ren asked me to write the foreword to this book almost six years before it took its final shape and revealed the story and message you will find in these pages. It dawns on me, as I type, that after so many years of knowing Ren, even I am catching up with what these years of evolution have yielded. This is not simply a book about how to engage with animals in a more respectful and undomesticated way, but how, through our relationship with the animals in our care, we can set in motion the momentum of our own undomestication; which is to say, a path of understanding and embodying our real power, potential, and love as human animals, outside of the systems, stories, and methods of captivity and exploitation that seek to reduce us every day.

The harder-to-swallow pill is admitting that we, ourselves, use those very same avenues to reduce each other and those in our care for our own benefit and false sense of love and belonging. No one is free until all are free, and emancipation is not merely something we seek, but also must grant. To understand that we contain the power to grant freedom and the chance for true maturation and evolution in another, through the love of honoring their innate capacity and power, is quite a thing.

I remember clearly the first time I sat down with Ren in a one-on-one session following one of my workshops in Ashland, Oregon. She quickly revealed the depth of her reach for truth, as well as the pain of distance she felt between where she was and what she not only yearned for but had faith was possible in herself and her life.

I knew peripherally, in 2015, that she was working with horses in a profound and brave way, was on the heels of an even more fully fleshed-out body of work, and that she found the work of somatic and elemental inhabitance I was offering— the remembering and reclaiming our deepest origins and potentials—inextricably connected with her work and dedication to animals. I also knew that she was inextricably dedicated to the path of her own becoming and freedom, and was willing to lean into incredible discomfort. Without ever naming it in that first session, we both knew that there was only one vessel that would ferry her across the ocean of this great unknown: the forever seaworthy vessel of vulnerability.

A few events, over many years, had to happen between her initial invitation and my sitting down to actually write this foreword, as we tip toward the light of spring in the Northern Hemisphere. She had to, of course, finish the book, which required living the book before it was written, from cover to cover, inside out, and I had to come into relationship as the guardian of a regal, feisty, and self-possessed pup named Filí. It is my months of caring for Filí under the guidance of principles in this book that allows me a more intimate understanding of the potential, healing, and power found in *The Wisdom of Wildness*, and I am keenly aware that I have barely begun to scratch the surface of what is possible.

No matter who we are and where we come from, two great inheritances have been bestowed upon us in this life: domestication and wildness. One is a mirage, a trick of the mind from a rendered state of exile and, therefore, desperation; the other is a wellspring that quenches to the bone.

The first, our domestication, is an overlay. It is a disembodied and dislocated jumble of socialization, conditioning, and interruption and amnesia, manipulation, commodification, and exploitation of the width of our humanity. It exists, as Ren speaks to, because of countless (and current) millennia and generations of human flight from emotional pain, trauma, denial, unaccountability, and disembodiment, and therefore, an unimaginable fragmentation of our wholeness.

Ren puts forth, through her decades of work with animals, one of the most powerful definitions and understandings of domestication I have ever encountered:

> she illuminates that domestication is a state of learned
> (taught, bought, forced) helplessness.

Please read that sentence again. Domestication is a state of learned helplessness. How many ways, in the exposure of that sentence, can we recognize how we have been conditioned into helplessness, a state of being that has us over-reaching in order to feel "okay"— pursuing bonds and activity forged from this ground of fundamental lack and dependence, rather than the embodied experience of our wholeness. By design, domestication casts a spell rendering us powerless, separate, unworthy, second-guessing, dependent, bound, captive…helpless.

If we want to know how this turns out, we need only turn toward the engine of perceived and believed helplessness that drives our systems of capitalism, racism, consumption, and commodification. It is a surefire equation for giving our power away to something outside of ourselves—be that a product, partner, job, guru, belief, or some far-flung future of hoped-for salvation that insulates us not only from our pain but from our true power.

We can all identify the ways in which we have been diminished by this state of learned helplessness. But, as I said, the uncomfortable angle to admit is that we, by way of this domestication, perpetuate, inflict, and expect that reduction in the bodies and lives of those with whom we are in relationship, in order to feel needed, wanted, loved, and of purpose. But remember, domestication is an overlay. That is good news. It is not who we really are.

Our other inheritance, our wildness, is our truest nature, our original skin. It is our innate, instinctual, intact essence and humanity—our very soul, if you will—which both embodies and expresses freedom. Our wildness is not something we have to earn or learn, for that matter. We revive it by way of remembering, uncovering, reclaiming, and allowing. This wildness is our birthright, a return to which is met first by waking up to the cost of our domestication: the capture, interruption, and exploitation of our God-given biointelligence, creative-potential, and the bone-known indivisibility of our human animality with all of life. Our innate wildness, in stark contrast to the learned helplessness of domestication, is truly powerful. It is emergent creation-force, pure potential, and the embodied wisdom-in-motion of life itself.

And secondly, we reclaim this wildness, by being vulnerable enough to listen, trust, ask, and see without interpretation, expectation, or over-lay. This wild instinct, intuition, messaging, and sense-making speaks to us in a language much more indigenous than our learned linguistic tongue. It speaks through the subtle somatic sensations and emotions we register in our cells as animal bodies. It speaks in the riddles and verse of the unseen world, and converses through a lush, private dia-logue between our deepest inner spaces and that which moves in and through all things.

Each time we turn toward this soul-sensed language and exchange, we relinquish the *terra firma* of the limited and known world of our conditioning and domestication and open to a much larger, more vital and life-giving conversation. We open to a true meeting with each other and the moment, and an intelligence that we can both give and receive. It is in this moment-to-moment sense-seeing that we have the chance to not only encounter our own emancipation but to grasp that freedom wherever we lend our gaze.

In your hands you hold a story and an invitation into a path and practice of undomestication, maturation, and return to wildness, with echoes and implications in 360 degrees. What I find fresh, exciting, humbling, and profound about *The Wisdom of Wildness* is that it is unequivocally where the rubber meets the road in the work of "rewild-ing." It is the grounded, tangible practice of undomesticating ourselves through our daily relationship with the pets and the animals in our care, the most obvious example of lives that would literally not exist without the inheritance and perpetuation of domestication.

What is true about these animals is that they will never be free from captivity, *just as most of us will never be free from interface with the infinite constructs of our modern world (from concrete and currency to electricity and clothing)*. What we can grant them is the maturation and sovereignty of their inner lives and emotional development, and a relationship in which we do not teach them helplessness in order for us to feel loved and whole. *What we, in turn, grant ourselves, is the chance to love, listen and communicate in a way that does not inflict emotional domestication and begins to hint at our true power, creative capacity and return to our own instincts and intuition.*

> Ren asks us to become humans that the wild wants to be near,
> and dares us to become the wild we admire.

Rarely do we give ourselves the chance to constellate life around us through our own energetic merits without some kind of strategizing or manipulation. In simple example, who would we have to become in order for animals to want to listen to and follow us without luring them with a bribe of a treat? What would happen to our own understanding of power if we realized that behavior modification and manipulation is not necessary to achieve harmonious relationship with animals (as well as children, partners, friends)? How would we relate and what would emerge in ourselves and our animals?

This rewilding is not philosophical or aspirational; it is a real-time journey in direct relationship with the instinctual nature of the wilder animal-bodies among us. They give us consistent, intuitive, perceptive, and accurate response and information in every moment, without fail—until we train it out of them, as it has been trained out of us; until we teach them that "well-behaved" and "compliant" takes precedence over instinctual intelligence and unique gift. Sound familiar?

Wildness is not out-of-control delinquency. It is embodied, resilient, and wise coherence that has an always present natural order if we can be vulnerable enough to risk exploring a way of being that is outside of our conditioning and more true to our nature.

In the seven years since first meeting Ren—a span of time that has never been without the writing and evolution of this book—I have had the honor of traveling alongside her as a mentor, be it near or far. Through countless hours of sacred physical practice and study, phone calls, storytelling, writing sessions, and weeks of time together in the wilderness, I have witnessed first-hand her willingness to burn in the fire, be dismantled, to let go, risk, trust, renounce, receive, and grow. I have been on the other end of the line in her moments of excruciating "writer's block," only for us to uncover that the next chapter of this book could not reveal itself until she had given herself to her next chapter in the cauldron of vulnerability, accountability, and healing and becoming, again and again, for years.

She started out writing one book only to find she was writing a different one, by way of a very personal inner passage and necessity. She took the very journey she is inviting us on, one that she both courted and was courted by. This book is not a mere yearning; it is a tried-and-true, field-tested synthesis of her courageous experiment of lived-experience and trust, surrender and soul emergence.

Though Ren has done a more than stellar job with her own words, I'd like to invite you into the adventure of these pages with the resounding faith that what you are seeking is already who you are; that you have the power to not only exist from a state of freedom, but to grant it. Quite literally, we are the change we seek. No one is free until all are free. May we begin together, again and again, and meet with love on the path.

~ Sarah Byrden
Writer, educator, and wilderness guide,
Santa Fe, New Mexico
www.theelementalself.com

INTRODUCTION

Transformation has a smell. For me, it is crisp desert air with a hint of sage, especially after a rain. That's when the aroma takes on a whole new identity, like a Phoenix rising from the tear-soaked ashes of grief. Naivety led me to believe that when the mystical bird plants her feet again, a new world surrounds her. It felt that way for some time, and remembering those days gives me a faith and strength that is untamed and unshakable. However, in such an intricately connected physical reality, it often takes many transitions before a person can reach metamorphosis.

Many changes are often needed to remain an outlier to conditioned beliefs pervading even the wisest among us. I really want to believe that someone can instantly walk away with the scars but not the old habits of a lifetime of conditioning, but for most of us, it takes practice and a lot of grieving.

Fortunately, there is one permanence in this life that we can always reach for to aid us through difficult change, and it isn't death or taxes; it's love, and not the love most of us were taught to believe in.

I originally learned the true nature of love through my relationship to horses, as told in my first book, *Riding on the Power of Others: A Horsewoman's Path to Unconditional Love* (Vegan Publishers, 2015). I highly recommend reading it if you want to know the history behind the book you're reading now. The story in the first book was told from the high desert of Northern California, where, unexpectedly, this story is also being told. A not-so-gentle guidance brought me back to this place, landing the horses and me only a few miles from where my first big shift occurred, and I've spent the last eight years dismantling myself again and again to bring these words to you.

I never intended to come back here, and I most definitely never fully understood the magic of this environment or why the desert has been so paramount for so many remarkable journeys of awakening. There is a stripping away of all things unnecessary that takes place here, where all distractions ultimately must end if one is to overcome the discomfort of such a harsh and challenging terrain. The desert doesn't aim to surround you with the lush reassurance of, say, a forest. No. Everything about this ecosystem invites the opportunity to help one find sanctuary within, and until that happens, the arms of this particular wilderness will not extend to embrace you. When you no longer reach for her from desperation, that's when she will arrive to care for you in ways far beyond those you were seeking. Love is like that, too.

We have become a domesticated society full of people and animals exploited for another's needs, even in our most intimate, personal relationships. The devastating result has been a worldwide forgetting of our true nature as well as the very meaning and power of love. Disconnection from one another has led to massive suffering and destruction all around our world, and we seem to be running out of time faster than ever before. Many of us unknowingly perpetuate this state of disconnection through the very relationships we seek out in order to feel connected. I'm here to help you authentically restore that connection and reclaim the deepest experience of love through your relationship to those who have modeled it for centuries: the animals we think of as family.

Love is what this story is about, and I'm writing it for anyone who has ever cared for or been loved by an animal. I know of no bigger motivator for lasting change than the desire to be free of pain. My life has been filled with immense suffering, and every bit of that suffering can be tied to some failure to love or be loved by another. However, nothing has ever hurt more than when I've discovered how I've caused harm to someone I cared for by failing to truly love them beyond my personal experience of them.

Real love is embodied in ways I have rarely witnessed outside of a wild setting. It is not a feeling, but a state of being through which no one is seen as outside of the whole. Love is wild, and somehow humanity has lost touch, and even become fearful, of what that word means.

After walking away from a successful career as a professional horse-woman, I lived for two years with an undomesticated herd of horses in the high desert wilderness. Free of any strong outside influences, I experienced the wild, unconditional nature of love long enough for it to change me forever. Most importantly, though, I learned what it really means to be domesticated, and how few of us are actually free from another's use and purpose.

Being domesticated creates a limited perspective of reality that keeps us from stepping into the fullness of who and what we really are. The term "domestication" literally means "to control in order to use"; it has little to do with biology, and far more to do with the manipulation of another's emotional experience. Sadly, many beings, human and nonhuman alike, are created for the purpose of meeting another's needs. When we are exploited for another's use, we are robbed of the inherent joy meant to guide us towards our individual and collective destinies. By learning how to undomesticate the herd of horses in my care, I began unraveling my own domestication and uncovering a path that has been leading me back to a power within myself I could not have imagined. However, the horses could only take me so far, because I could choose when and how I interacted with them too easily. It was not until I turned my attention toward those sharing my home and living by my side that deeper answers were revealed.

Those who have read my first book are often horrified at the abuse that is so prevalent within the horse industry, conducted by well-meaning people like myself. I am not at all proud to say that my use of dogs goes beyond anything revealed in that first book. My deepest shame did not come from my history with horses. As a young person, I used horses to feel powerful and in control of my life. It was relatively easy for me to look back at my childhood and find understanding and compassion around that, which also made it easy to reveal in my story. Dogs represent a much larger body of pain for me. I have also used dogs for power and control, but for as long as I can remember, I used them to feel safe and to feel loved in a world in which I didn't feel worthy.

While the body of work presented in this book can be applied equally to all species and relationships, I'm going to take you along on my journey with an incredible dog named Denali. Every other chapter will carry you through my experience with her, interwoven with chapters on the more philosophical aspects of an evolving understanding of love and trauma. *Riding on the Power of Others: A Horsewoman's Path to*

Unconditional Love was the what; this sequel offers the why and how. It took much longer to write. Facing the truth of what we do to those we care about the most has been the scariest, most painful process I have ever been through. To look at my love for dogs through a more mature lens was not easy. My hope is that my example and the information that follows can help you avoid some of that pain on your own path.

A rewilding of our planet is underway, carried forth by those courageous enough to peel back the layers of their own conditioning. I believe that our collective relationship to animals is one of the biggest obstacles—if not the biggest obstacle—keeping us from a balanced, interconnected existence on Earth. Each one of us has the power to turn it around, beginning in our own homes. The great poet Rumi spoke of a field beyond right and wrong. That field is the wilderness, and this book is an invitation to meet me there.

PART ONE

>>>⊙<<<

SEEK TRUTH

Chapter 1
ORIGINAL SIN

The hunt had been a great success. Led by the female they had loyally followed for the past six years, the pack had been tracking the old bull for days. Finally, weakened from age and the wolves' endless pursuit, the animal stumbled and was down just long enough for instinct to initiate the direct attack. The actual killing she could handle on her own, but the strength of the pack made the moment possible. With the matriarch at his throat, the bull was taking his last breath before any of the other wolves even sunk their teeth into him.

As the pack gorged themselves on their kill, the leader's attention was persistently pulled back toward the den where her young pups had been left in the care of two of their older siblings. She ate feverishly, engulfing as much as she could hold to meet both her own needs and the needs of her cubs. Her packmates did the same. Their family bond was strong, and the development and survival of each litter was a shared responsibility.

The white fur that normally provided camouflage in the snowy landscape was now glistening red from her nose to her shoulders, all the way down to her front paws. A pack this large could easily defend their meal. Confidence, however, lay in having a leader that had proven herself repeatedly to neighboring territories. This landscape was governed by her and her kin with the fierce commitment and skill passed down by generations of worthy leaders before her. The pack had called this place home for years without fear. That is, until the arrival of man.

The wolves weren't sure what to make of the two-legged predators that smelled more like prey, other than to proceed with extreme caution. Often, in recent times, the men could be seen observing the wolves and even mimicking their hunting behavior. Only, the men never got too close to the animals they pursued—they used trickery and things beyond the wolves' understanding to kill from a distance. The pack had learned not to get too close after the first of them to become curious, their patriarch, was impaled with a sharp stick months ago. With her mate dead and no new pups on the way until she could find another suitable partner, the alpha female was anxious to return to her brood.

Sleep was necessary that night to prepare for the journey home, but she stirred repeatedly from some unknown concern. Some rest was better than none, at least, and another huge meal the next morning gave the pack the strength they needed to head back. A few inches of fresh powder had been added to the snowpack overnight, and as the wolves made their way back into the forest, there was a single-file line of fresh prints leading away from the remains left for others to feed upon. Seemingly less pertinent than the immediate needs of their own pack, the ravens had descended before the last wolf was out of sight. Every kill made served the entire community they were a part of. They maintained the balance of whatever land they occupied, the keepers of the wild.

Stopping only to drink, what would otherwise be a joyful return was increasingly becoming filled with urgency as the alpha led them faster and faster toward home. Something was wrong. Something was very, very wrong, but what could it be? No other known predator in this forest would dare lay claim to her den with the legacy that had protected it for more than three generations. Her mother and grandmother shared the same white coat, both as fierce and protective an alpha as she now was. Unless a rogue pack had emerged in the area from far away, whatever threat she was chasing must be new. If another pack had appeared, they likely would have at least heard a warning call from those left guarding the pups.

She smelled the blood first, then she smelled the men. Worn weary from their travels and the hunt, the she-wolf found a second wind that only the need to protect could provoke, and the pack surged toward home at record speed. What they came upon when they arrived at the mouth of the den stopped everyone in their tracks. Except for her. Beyond the need to assess, she dashed past the bloodied, furless carcasses of her older children and straight into the den.

When she heard the howls begin outside, she knew there was no hope. The pups were gone. With an enormously full belly of food for her missing offspring, she slowly emerged from the hole, weighted down with something far heavier than digesting flesh. The scent of the men was strong, but the scent of the pups' struggle even stronger. It was clear that they had been taken. The pack had seen the strange two-legged animals hunt enough to know not to pursue them. They could attack from a distance with teeth on the end of flying sticks, and the wolves would not stand a chance against a pack of them. All they could do was mourn their dead and lost and wake up the next day to a life that goes on.

Miles from the den, the children of men were laughing joyfully while they curiously pursued and attempted to play with their new companions; a budding relationship heavily reliant upon strips of raw meat for encouragement, punishment for undesirable behavior, and the influence and confines of captivity. Meanwhile, in the distance, a lone, melancholy howl echoed hollowly through the night.

⊙≫⊙≪⊙

Chapter 2
THE WISDOM OF THE WILD

The consciousness that resides within every living being never questions the interconnectedness of all life. It is awareness beyond mind and form, unable to be claimed, yet available to all. Such connection is ineffable. It cannot be understood by the mind, yet there is a knowing. It cannot be felt in the body, but the body is its messenger. Informing through instinct, intuition, and inspiration, it is the grounded, embodied experience of being one with spirit and all that is while still operating independently as the animals we are designed to be. To be fully engaged with this connection is what it means to be wild. To allow it to guide one's path is to be granted access to the wisdom of the soul.

Each one of us comes to Earth with purpose. Trying to define that purpose in words will not get us closer to it, nor will thinking of it as an end goal or destination. True purpose is lived in each moment, allowing intrinsic motivation to guide us toward ultimate destiny. Inspiration can only be birthed through the connection to soul that began and remains wild within each of us. This connection is how we know what we must do to be fulfilled in our lives. It is the most important intelligence an Earthling can access, and yet, those with the simplest of minds are usually the wisest to it. Only humans, it seems, have the audacity to challenge nature's design.

What makes someone wild is not necessarily their biology or where they live, but rather, the degree to which they have been able to fully emotionally mature. In other words, a truly wild animal, human or otherwise, is one that has learned how to feel and internally process emotion to a degree that those feelings become subtle and deeply personal information for the feeler, rather than something to be expressed, projected, sought out, or avoided due to trauma. Trauma, then, is not necessarily an event, but the interference in emotional development. When energy is able to move through us freely, there is no longer an obstacle to wild wisdom. This is why even the most domesticated among us can have profound experiences of connection, as long as, in those moments, nothing is present to trigger any unresolved emotional trauma. When the energy flows, the connection is clear. A full restoration of that connection through a process of "rewilding" means we no longer have to seek out those experiences; instead, being deeply connected becomes the normal experience of what it means to be a wild, human animal.

This book, and this work, can help you reclaim your own wild nature, regardless of whether you live off the grid or in a luxury Manhattan apartment. Your wild never left you, and I intend to help you find it by teaching you how to witness the wolf in your dog. Chihuahuas have the same access to wild wisdom that gray wolves do. Their ability to stay connected to it has far more to do with their relationship to us than to their biology, even if we've set the Chihuahua up to fail at ever achieving full blown autonomy. However, what we can give the Chihuahua is the opportunity to establish emotional sovereignty, and subsequently model for us, often faster than we can achieve it ourselves, what it looks like to be emotionally whole. That is what it means to be wild.

For far too long, the "wild" has been something used to strike fear into our hearts as a concept more relatable to danger and recklessness than wisdom. In our desire to become civilized and supposedly more advanced in social and cultural development, we've moved too far away from our wild roots to realize the harm we're causing to ourselves, each other, and the planet we all call home. I can think of more than a few reasons why those with tremendous external power would want things to remain this way, but it is not sustainable and serves only a few.

We need to rebalance the system in service to all.

When a system with seemingly separate parts behaves holistically, there can only be an overall harmony maintained through that balance. Those who behave independently through abuses of power become an anomaly to the system, wreaking havoc on the health of our shared environment. Interconnection is what keeps a natural system in balance.

We are individual, physical forms having both a unique and shared experience through a unified consciousness that exists beyond form. In other words, we are not completely separate and cannot behave as if we are without grave consequence. The moment we lose touch with our connection to one another, we risk playing God without God consciousness. When we are not being guided by what connects us, our choices contribute to the only sin that has ever existed: believing and behaving as if we are completely separate from Source, and each other. Immeasurable fear and suffering is the result of such widespread experience.

Our bodies are the doorway to freedom; our intuition the most reliable intelligence. Healthy, mature wild animals model this through their present, embodied example of emotional awareness. They have no reason to question that we are all one at an energetic level, because that is the primary way they experience the world around them: through feeling as opposed to thought. Our own species has managed to reverse the priority, allowing the mind to rule over that for which it was intended to be merely a tool. No matter where we live, the wilderness of our internal landscape remains. As long as we fear the wild and what it has to show us, we will continue to move farther and farther from the connection that makes us whole.

The wisdom of the wild is the unexplainable knowledge we gain by staying connected to our soul through our feeling body. It informs beyond ideas of right and wrong in ways that would never inspire unnecessary harm to others, our environment, or ourselves. This wisdom links us to a holistic understanding of our place in the physical world and is vitally important for the health of our planet and her inhabitants. We all have this link when we enter the world. I believe the explanation for how it goes missing can be found in the absence of exploitation among wild creatures. One cannot remain authentically connected to someone they are deeming separate enough to use.

Chapter 3
GODDESS OF DEATH

The first time I thought I saw a white wolf, I was driving down a dirt road on my way to work. The "wolf" was bounding across a large, open pasture, headed right for the section of road I was about to reach. As she ducked under the fence, her icy-blue eyes met mine, piercing straight through my thoughts. Both my mind and my truck rolled to a dead stop in the middle of the road. She clearly wasn't a wolf, though she did look the part, and for the feelings she stirred inside me, she might as well have been.

I sat for a moment, just staring at the beautiful, solid-white husky. She had also stopped and was now looking directly into my eyes with a gentle confidence most dogs do not possess. I began to wonder what she was doing out here and where she belonged. Our gaze was interrupted when my companion in the passenger seat piped up, "Don't even think about it." My compulsion may not have been obvious to someone who didn't know me as well, but to the woman in the next seat, it was clear that I was working out how to take this dog home. I answered with an innocent-sounding "What?" and followed it with, "It's not like I would just take someone's dog." I slowly pulled away, leaving the dog where she stood. She may have been left standing by the side of the road, but some part of her followed me home that afternoon.

About a year passed, and I had picked up a new hoof care client in that same rural neighborhood. One afternoon, while I was bent over trimming hooves, my face was assaulted with wet tongue kisses. I giggled, and as I looked up, was shocked to see the same white husky under the horse with me, slowly wagging her tail and looking right into my eyes with that soft intensity I remembered. "That one is wild," my client said, followed with, "and she needs a new home." My heart skipped a beat. Apparently, she belonged next door to the people who owned the pasture I saw her in a year previous. They called her Kali, and the woman who claimed her was at her wits' end about what to do with her. Kali had lethal ambitions for several neighbors' chickens and smaller livestock, and a few people had threatened to shoot her if they saw her again. Clearly, she needed to be rescued, and that day, I just happened to be wearing my cape.

After ignoring cautioning glares and words from the other human member of my household, I arranged to pick up Kali a few days later. This time, in the passenger seat beside me rode Spur, my most loyal companion since the day of his birth four years earlier. His corgi mix mother, Pippa, had hooked up with a full-blooded Australian cattle dog after her very first, very unexpected heat, before I was able to prevent it. I returned home from town one day to find a puddle of puppies near the pillows on my bed. Picking up a little orange-colored squirmer from the pile, I declared out loud, "This is Spur, and we're keeping him."

Spur was my constant companion, so his opinion on the addition of a wolf to our pack was important to me. Maybe I just needed him beside me. Either way, I remember the grin on his face and the brightness in his eyes as he rode shotgun on the way to pick up the new girl. There was never an adventure he didn't seem excited to join me on, but as I opened the door for him to hop out and meet her, a flash of fear ran through him. Without hesitation, she attacked. Briefly horrified, I pulled her off him quickly, and everything neutralized. I had never met a dog that didn't love Spur, and even though they were fine with one another after that initial incident, I could not shake the feeling that I had just witnessed something important I couldn't quite name. In any case, fate seemed as good a scapegoat as any for bad decision-making.

Everything on the outside said that I was making a huge mistake, but something on the inside told me that I needed this dog in my life. Maybe it was because I'd been obsessed with wanting a white husky ever since I saw the Disney film *Iron Will* as a child, but there was a deeper element to the longing than any movie could have caused. It is said that the Hindu goddess Kali brings death to the ego as the illusory, self-centered view of reality. She is the life-giver, preserver, and destroyer, whose name means "she who is death." I wonder if I might have chosen differently that day had I known how much death was approaching. At least I had the good sense to change her name.

My obsession with wolves started early. Even as a child, the unconscious pull toward my own wild freedom filled me with wonder any time I read of wolves in books or saw them in movies. At the age of 15, my bedroom was not plastered with teen idols or bands, but *canis lupus* in every color phase. One wall was a collage of every wolf picture, poster, or calendar photo I could get my hands on, and my bedspread and blankets depicted their images as well. I dreamed of moving to Montana to track and research wolves in the wild, but those were dreams for a girl who didn't carry the wounds of my childhood. Instead, my trauma led me onto the backs of horses, where I found a coping mechanism that would keep my deepest longings at bay for years. The still, small voice inside me got harder and harder to hear through the thundering of hooves keeping me safe from emotional pain.

Despite not pursuing my dream of becoming a wolf biologist, my heart couldn't forget the passion I had for the wild or the animals that remained that way. In the summer of 2010, I leapt at the opportunity to take my first trip to Alaska, and there, I saw more wild than I had ever known in my entire life. Inspiration filled my lungs as I gazed at the more than 20,000-foot-high summit of Denali, but there was so much sadness inside me, the inspiration quickly transformed into tears. I seethed with envy and shame when I looked at the young women with hiking and climbing gear I didn't have a clue how to use or the money to possess, as I longed desperately for a life other than the one I was living.

Earlier that morning, on the bus up to the viewing station, one of my dreams came true. A lone male wolf crossed onto the road ahead, and we stopped to take photos. At last, I was finally seeing a real, wild wolf in the wilderness. As I raised the camera to my face, he stopped and turned his head to look right at me, then he hiked his leg to piss on the tree beside him. There was zero fear present in him as he stared back at a busload of humans and laid claim to what was his. He owned the wild in ways that were lost on me in that moment, but I will never forget his expression. It was the most unapologetic, confident display I had ever witnessed, and as he loped off into the Alaskan bush, I wondered what it would feel like to know and accept oneself so fully.

A few months later, I was driving home with a fluffy, white wolf look-alike I had decided to rename Denali, after the majestic mountain I had stood in awe of in Alaska. She wasn't exactly wild, but she was the closest to it I had ever seen in a dog, and I wanted a piece of whatever that was.

It never occurred to me to look inside myself when it was so easy to claim others as my own. Denali was incredibly brave and smart, confident and beautiful, and on some level I must have believed that making her mine would get me a little closer to those things as well. What I wouldn't have believed is how much chaos could be created by trying to possess someone who refused to be owned.

It took no time at all to realize what I was up against in trying to contain this monster of a dog. Keeping Denali fenced in was no joke, and she was quickly becoming my worst nightmare in dog guardianship. She had zero respect for my so-called authority. Feral in many ways, she had simply known freedom too intimately to live by another's rules. From puppyhood on, she had grown up in an expansive rural neighborhood with plenty of room to run, and plenty of local fowl to desecrate. Every effort I made to contain her was met with an almost sinister stare before she would then turn her attention on whatever boundary was to be her new challenge.

Denali would sit and quietly calculate her plans to such a degree that even the most serious skeptic would have had a hard time arguing for the cognitive limitations of animals. You could watch her observing her surroundings, and the second your attention was off her, she would spring into quick, efficient action and be gone before you knew what had happened. Her ability to detect weakness in her environment was uncanny. A six-foot-high privacy fence might as well have been a wall of bubbles for how effective it was at keeping her in.

Denali could climb, jump, or dig her way out of just about anything as long as she could do it without seriously hurting herself. I didn't want to hurt her, and I was beginning to think it would take a small fortune to contain her.

I decided to try leaving her in the house. Big mistake. The first time I did this, I walked into the kitchen to find a very bright-eyed husky, tongue lolling, and every single cabinet door standing open, as well as the refrigerator, with empty packages strewn about from anything and everything she had decided to devour.

No big deal, I told myself, just secure things a bit better—except that didn't work, either. The next time I attempted to leave her inside when I went away, I came home to several hundred dollars' worth of trashed blinds, topped off with a busted-out window above the kitchen sink that she had decided to use as an emergency exit. The dog had no regard for the boundaries I was imposing, and the more I tried to control her, the more she retaliated and made my life hell.

I thought that taking her for long walks might help, but walking Denali was like being towed behind a pickup truck. I didn't have the time or space or clarity in my life to give her what she needed, or even know what that was.

It was becoming obvious that I had made a big mistake in bringing her home.

This became my life until one afternoon after yet another escape. I heard a gunshot from a neighboring property. My heart sank, as I just knew it had to do with her. A few minutes later, running full speed toward home, she jumped the fence to return to the back yard. She was covered in blood.

Chapter 4
THE ROOT OF SEPARATION

I remember the moment clarity finally landed. It was 2013, and I was in Ashland, Oregon, to hear don Miguel Ruiz and his son, don Miguel Ruiz, Jr., speak about the son's upcoming book, *The Five Levels of Attachment*. Having read most of their previous books, including don Miguel Ruiz's original *The Four Agreements*, I was already aware of the beautiful way in which they both articulate the domestication of humanity, but it wasn't until I was in the audience that day that I made the connection between our own domestication and that which we inflict on others.

The domestication of other animals was not questioned on the stage that day, but as I listened to them speak about humanity's affliction, it became glaringly obvious to me why so many people (specifically, animal lovers) remain stuck in their own conditioning. That evening, I also found the words for what I was really doing with my horses: undomesticating them. It wasn't a big leap, then, to realize there is simply no way to fully undomesticate our own lives while directly engaging in the domestication of others. Domestication begets domestication. I seriously doubt we will ever know when or where it all really began, but I believe to my core that understanding the underlying nature of domestication, and moving away from it, is the missing piece to humanity's collective evolution. Without that, there is little chance of restoring balance to our planet.

Domestication, with regard to how it is used in my work and within these pages, means to control and condition another for use. It isn't as simple as merely using direct forms of control, such as physical abuse, which require much less skill than the more dangerous forms. Domestication requires manipulation in the form of influencing someone's emotional experience to control their behavior (think, marketing and advertising). I became an expert in such behavior through nearly 20 years of professional horse training. The only way to control someone through emotion is to take advantage of their domestication. The only way to set someone free is to reverse-engineer the process.

Domesticating someone usually involves systems of reward and punishment and always results in some level of learned helplessness. It involves intentionally interrupting someone's emotional experience in order to redirect it somewhere more desirable for whoever is in a position of power within the relationship dynamic. Deeply connected, emotionally mature beings are not susceptible to emotional or psychological control, and that is what makes them dangerous to a cultural framework that is highly dependent upon domestication.

Domesticating others involves interrupting their early emotional development. This is why truly wild animals are so difficult, if not impossible, to tame. One may be able to train/control an immature biological tiger, but trying to take a fully developed wild tiger out of the wilderness and control them is almost unheard of. An emotionally mature, wild animal, human or otherwise, would never allow such attempts at control, nor would they be a reasonable target for such. The exception is when an animal appears to be wild biologically but has suffered a trauma that has left them vulnerable to undue influence. We cannot judge one's wildness on biology alone; we must understand the level of emotional maturity that has been achieved.

Trauma is the fundamental root of separation. Trauma is not what happens to us, but rather, any interruption in an emotional process that goes unresolved, thereby stunting our ability to fully process that particular emotion. The presence of emotional triggers indicates that we are not yet mature enough to handle particular emotions; once we are, triggers all but disappear and emotions become a more subtle, informative experience.

Healing from trauma, therefore, is really about becoming emotionally mature as opposed to coming to terms with some event in our lives. A parent's consistent criticism is enough to domesticate a human child. In the wild, most offspring are raised in an unconditional manner that very much supports their full emotional development, but sometimes events happen to disrupt nature's design. For example, if the emotionally mature members of a wild animal family suddenly die, there is no one left to teach the less mature animals. They may then carry that trauma into survival behaviors that may or may not reflect the natural behavior of their species. A good example of this is a scenario whereby humans kill the mature members of a wolf pack and orphan the immature wolves. Those that are then left to lead lack the emotional development and wisdom to do so, causing them to behave in ways that may not be aligned with their more mature intended design. "Survival mode" becomes the norm, and reckless action may be taken because one is disconnected from a deeper intrinsic guidance.

All addictions and most mental health disorders are the result of trauma, and domestication is the most widespread form of trauma in our world. It is the act of literally separating someone from their soul's communication in order to use them for personal benefit. Emotion is the language of the soul, and trauma is the obstacle to receiving its message. The only reason we would ever domesticate another being is because we ourselves have been separated from our own soul by trauma. This cycle of trauma within the human species, on a vast spectrum of experience, has been our prevailing paradigm for longer than recorded history. Very few humans have any understanding of what it even means to be without their own domestication. What the original trauma of our species was, we can only hypothesize, but why it continued seems clear. It is a lot easier to control others in an attempt to avoid discomfort and pain than to use pain and discomfort as guiding forces in our lives. The cost, however, is our freedom and potential.

From the moment we enter this world, those who have forgotten their own true nature begin to mold us into something less than what we are. There is no value in feeling shame in this, as we are, individually and collectively, all victims of centuries of deeply ingrained social conditioning. Often even before birth, we are assigned a name and placed directly on a path of unconscious limitation, being indoctrinated, even innocently so, by our parents, extended family, teachers, and community. Government and society then form the framework for the perpetuation of eons of oppression and denial. In addition, we are repeatedly fed the importance of community and human interaction. When the only humans readily available to commune with are those in a deep state of similar conditioning themselves, this presents a real conundrum for remembering why we're here and how interconnected we actually are.

Knowing when, why, and how domestication began may not be possible. I do find it concerning that the most widely believed first story of man describes woman being made from man for man, but let's just look back to where things get a bit more obvious. For most people, the word domestication is most relatable to animals. Domestication is the same concept, no matter to whom it is applied, but the domestication of other animals, especially, may be the single most egregious error in human history. No other act has separated, and continues to separate, us farther from the natural world than our decision to enslave this very world.

While it isn't known for sure, many experts agree that wolves were the first animals to be domesticated by man, at least 14,000 years ago. Romanticism often surrounds the concept of "man's best friend" and the so-called symbiotic relationship that ensued to put dogs by our sides today.

An interesting story supported by many dog "lovers" theorizes that the first wolves to enter the camps of men more or less domesticated themselves in exchange for food, protection, and companionship. There is one huge flaw to that story: Symbiotic relationships are not born from abuses of power, and domestication cannot occur outside of exploitation. Exploitation always involves an abuse of power to serve the desires of the abuser, even if the relationship has mutual benefits.

The more likely scenario of the first domestication of wolves would look like capturing young pups and forcing them into captivity to serve humans. At minimum, it would look like a transactional relationship involving food, whereby at some point a line was crossed to implement permanent control over the animal.

Using the word "slave" to describe the relationship may be unsettling to those who enjoy the companionship of animals; however, the simple definition of a slave is one who is subject to control by another and forced to obey. Such is the nature of pet ownership, no matter how you spin it, even when the slaves are incredibly well cared for and adored. While I realize it may not be easy to consider, since the trauma of our own domestication results in very intense emotional experiences we are unprepared to process, exploitation forms the basis for the vast majority of humanity's relationship to animals. This isn't a hard concept to understand. It is, however, a very uncomfortable thing to feel and consider while caring for a beloved, dependent animal and using a domesticated understanding of love as justification for their care.

Domestication may be the root of why so many humans experience such a huge gap between their physical existence and their spiritual one. Our use of one another, and therefore practical denial of our fundamental connection to said other, keeps most of us from ever stepping beyond connection in theory or fleeting experience and into a lifetime of knowing. When our behavior is out of alignment with our actual beliefs and values it creates cognitive dissonance. Repeating the same experiences of cognitive dissonance can keep us stuck and unable to evolve if we are unable to close the integrity gap that has been created as a result.

Amazingly, a solution to our separation can be found by circling back to the animals many of us consider family: our animal kin. For as long as I can remember, I surrounded myself with animals to feel okay in the world. Animals were safe, they were consistent, and to a large degree they could be controlled and guaranteed to provide the comfort I sought from them. I needed them for my very survival as a young person navigating the unstable environment of a home riddled with trauma. I would give anything to have learned sooner what a dangerous drug my emotional use of animals would turn out to be, as I grew and moved into intimate relationships with other humans. Nothing in my life has caused more suffering than attachment to others for my own emotional stability.

It took a stallion with very clear boundaries and some stepping way outside my comfort zone for me to learn what real love is all about. Shai showed me just how important it is for anyone who wants to remain wild to understand the unconditional nature of love. As a result, and to thank him for the most important lesson I ever learned, I signed a lifetime contract to love all animals the way they had always loved me. It is the same unspoken agreement between all wild creatures and those in their care; an agreement to uphold every individual's right to personal emotional sovereignty.

⊙›››⊙‹‹‹⊙

Chapter 5

INSTINCT

A thorough inspection of Denali's blood-stained fur revealed no sign of injury to her body. That could only mean one thing: Any relief I felt for her well-being quickly subsided as I realized that the blood must have come from another animal. I knew I had brought home a killer, but this was definitely too much blood to be from a chicken.

I was at a complete loss. She was clearly too much for me to handle, and it was literally costing lives. Not knowing where she had been, and having several neighbors with large plots of land around us, I just walked with her to the front porch to sit and wait. Any moment there would be a truck tearing up my driveway to accuse my murderous husky.

No one showed. The phone didn't ring. I sat and waited for a long time hoping and not hoping to hear from someone who would reveal the facts so I could make amends for my dog's rampage.

Eventually, I retired, feeling guilty, confused, anxious, and completely overwhelmed about what to do next. I didn't know my neighbors, as I had only recently moved in, so I didn't have their phone numbers. The last thing I wanted to do was drive or walk up some long, private country drive to ask some stranger if my dog had killed anyone. Instead, I took immediate action to prevent any future assassinations. A weekend's worth of work and around a thousand dollars later, I had a dog kennel that could contain a tiger—maybe. It held Denali well enough, though, with its concrete floor and electrified fence-top perimeter.

Four days after Denali returned home in her red fur coat, the phone finally rang. One of my neighbors was calling to ask if I could come over to help his wife look for their llamas. Apparently, the day Denali had come home covered in blood, he had seen her chasing the llamas and fired off a warning shot, thankfully, that sent her straight home as intended. He also let me know where the blood had come from. Their female llama had recently delivered a stillborn baby, and for whatever reason, they left the carcass out in the open, attracting predators—predators like Denali. She had found the birth site and had been rolling in afterbirth and snacking on some of the remains. When the other llamas arrived to defend the body, Denali gave chase, and that's when the neighbor fired the gun to scare her off. Since then, the llamas had been missing.

At first I was relieved, then I arrived at the neighbor's property and uncovered a horrific scene. It was easy to determine that Denali had not, in fact, killed anyone, but it seems that she had played a key role in some unfortunate deaths. I found a yearling llama drowned in their stock pond, and I found the mother llama dead on a path. She had no obvious external wounds that could have caused her death, but it seemed unlikely that my dog had not been involved. Four days later it was pretty hard to know exactly what had happened, and it was even harder to understand how the neighbors had been unable to locate the bodies or why they had waited so long to reach out.

When I went back to their home to inform them of what I had found, I was met at the door by a woman on the edge of hysterics over the loss of her "beloved pets." I knew keeping my dog contained was my responsibility, and I felt horrible for whatever role she had played in their deaths, but the whole thing seemed bizarre. These animals had not even been checked on for days following the incident, and the dead baby was left openly attracting any and every creature that might be lured by the smell of blood. It was the first time I remember noticing the often enormous gap between someone's spoken love for the animals in their care and their actual behavior.

We made a reconciliation agreement that I was happy to honor, but I found myself being deeply judgmental toward my neighbors about their role in how the situation had unfolded —so consumed with judgment, in fact, that I was unable to see the reflection being offered in regard to my own choices.

The difficulty surrounding my life with Denali was heavily influenced by what was happening in my life with horses at that time. I had become a reasonably successful horse trainer and farrier, and Denali arrived near the end of my training days when I was already experiencing enough upheaval as a result of the change with horses. Less than a year after bringing her home, I had taken in a neglected stallion, Shai, who had completely upended my understanding of love and relationship in a way that made continuing to train animals impossible for me. However, I hadn't learned how or begun to apply what I was learning with horses to the other areas of my life. The universality of what I was beginning to understand was not yet accessible.

Any attempts to walk Denali on a lead happened in my pastures because I was too embarrassed to allow her to drag me down public sidewalks. The confusion and frustration inside me was enormous. I knew how to modify her behavior through training, but something deep inside me was telling me to find another way, just as I had for Shai and the other horses. I refused to force or manipulate her in order to earn her cooperation, and because it was all so new, my brain couldn't compute what the alternative would look like for dogs. I remember feeling consumed by thoughts of failure and the idea that I might never be able to enjoy a relationship with the dog I just had to "save," only to make her a prisoner in a 300-square-foot cage. Any progress in our relationship came to a complete standstill, and she remained in her kennel any time I could not keep a close eye on her.

Denali's eventual prison break resulted from the momentous decision to sell almost everything I owned and move across the country to create sanctuary for my horses. I had decided to leave the horse industry behind, and life as I knew it, after experiencing a deep shift in consciousness in relationship to the animals I had used to earn my paycheck for the previous 15 years. There's a different book for that story, but by the tail end of it, this one was concurrently unfolding.

In July 2013, I loaded up Denali and my three cowboy corgis (corgi/ heeler mixes) into a 19-foot-long RV and hit the road, trading 30 years of Texas roots for the high desert unknown of extreme Northern California. There, I began to undomesticate my life in ways I never could have imagined. Unfortunately, Denali was still way ahead of me in that regard. Our new life looked very similar to camping full time, completely off-grid in a remote and wild environment, and my misery with the white husky reignited. Without my fancy dog kennel, I was back at square one with Denali. It was actually more like negative square one because all I had was a small RV to call home for two humans, four dogs, and two cats.

If you're wondering if that was as bad as it sounds, it was. I was once more in way over my head, suddenly immersed in a lifestyle I was both unprepared for and ignorant about, and in a very harsh environment at that. I also happened to be going through a serious existential crisis and period of grief surrounding losing my identity as a professional horsewoman. I was in no position to keep tabs on the unruly husky I was basically having to keep on a lead at all times when we weren't in the "house" together. If she wasn't on a lead or in the RV with me, you can bet I was out looking for her all over what may as well have been an alien planet. Fortunately, everyone who meets Denali falls in love with her, so in my complete state of overwhelm, I allowed a new local friend to become her guardian. Following that decision, I felt the broken-hearted relief of releasing the burden of responsibility.

Life without Denali was so much easier. I despaired over letting her go, but the three corgis were well within the range of what I could reasonably manage at the time, and the relief I felt quickly outweighed my guilt or sadness. The woman who took her adored her, and I truly believed at that time that Denali was in far better hands than mine. We had not even closed or moved onto the property I had purchased when I gave up Denali, so imagine my surprise when one morning, weeks after being husky-free and finally finding some sanity, I looked up to see a large, white animal floating gracefully toward me in the distance across the desert landscape. My first thought was wondering if coyotes could be white. Then I felt brief excitement over the idea that it might possibly be a wolf. They were slowly making a comeback in that area, after all. I was shocked at the instant joy I experienced when I realized it was Denali. Somehow, without having ever been to that property before, she had found me.

I called her new guardian and let her know where she was, and I returned her after spending some time catching up and loving on her, all the while feeling a heaviness in my heart. I found out that she had been escaping just as much from her new home as she had with me, despite her new guardian's claims that it wouldn't happen under her care. She had even been picked up by law enforcement on one occasion! I was disappointed and concerned, but it still seemed pretty clear that I was in no position to take care of her myself. A few days later, Denali came back, and again, I was oddly thrilled to be reunited. This time, when I called to arrange her return, I was told in a cold tone that clearly she wanted to be with me, and I should probably just keep her. So I did.

For a significant period of my life, the biggest stress of the day could be summed up in the words, "Where's Denali?!" Circumstances went from difficult to very difficult overnight, as I now had to juggle learning how to survive out there with keeping track of the wild dog again. I felt the weight of responsibility, but I was also happy to have another chance to do right by her. It was a chance I was utterly failing at left and right, but I was determined to figure it out.

She ran off so much and so often, I just wanted to give up. I wasn't worried about her in the wild. She was an absolute pro at surviving and navigating the natural world. I just didn't want her to attack any domesticated animals, get shot, or get picked up by someone who didn't have her best interests in mind. I was more than open to finding her a better home, but there is a reason dogs like Denali end up dead or in shelters more often than not. Very few people take on a husky having any clue what the real requirements will be, and like I was at that time, far too many people are chasing wild wolf dreams as opposed to being responsible human beings.

I did not yet have the skills to keep up with Denali on foot. Thankfully, just a few months before deciding to move to California, I had traded in my two-wheel-drive truck for a four-wheel-drive SUV, having no idea at the time how much I would need such a versatile vehicle in the immediate future. After about the millionth time of chasing down Denali in my Toyota 4Runner, I noticed something interesting: I could always find her. We lived in a vast, unpopulated, and wild landscape, but somehow, some guidance I could not explain or fully understand would always help me find her, in ways I could not even begin to wrap my head around. As stressful as it all was, it started to fascinate me. How was I locating Denali? Were we communicating? Was my body leading me in ways my head could not? All of it was new, sometimes scary, and always exciting.

Chapter 6
THE GUARDIAN CONTRACT

There is a very specific container required for the emotional development of physical beings. The container is love, and it is absolutely unconditional. When pure, authentic love is offered to a developing being, it does not take long for the soul to fully integrate with the physical body and communication between the two to be established through emotion.

Unfortunately, only wild animals offer this unconditional container to their offspring. A wolf does not bear pups with an idea of who they should become. They simply model behavior, provide, protect, set boundaries, and allow the pups to follow where their own wild wisdom takes them. Having the pups was instinctual, based on the body's deeply informed "yes" rather than a preconceived idea.

Domesticated humans take a different approach, often planning the conditioning of their offspring, even before conception, and sometimes in great detail too. At least as common would be reproducing with no awareness of the body's cycles, resulting in accidental pregnancies. The most common motivation for both scenarios? Seeking personal satisfaction.

When a dependent is exploited by their primary caregiver(s), it fractures or delays the emotional maturation process that would otherwise create a fully functional adult animal. In order for a dependent to grow into a healthy, autonomous being, they must receive enough unconditional love and modeling to develop their own emotional intelligence. This love looks more like present, boundaried attention than mere kindness or affection. In that presence, one is offered the space to learn how to feel and process the full spectrum of emotion, connecting them to the intrinsic wisdom of their soul—their wild wisdom.

Obviously, that kind of space can only be offered by one who is emotionally aware and mature themselves. The very nature of why domesticated humans choose to create dependency in others, be it captive animals or their own offspring, makes it impossible for those in their care to fully establish this vital connection.

Are we hardwired for connection? Absolutely. However, most people are seeking external connection for the experience of what they are actually longing for inside and beyond themselves—the deep, eternal connection to their own soul.

We look everywhere for a taste of it, except where it's always been. Connection is found on the inside, just below all of the pain we've been avoiding. This pain would never have become such an enormous obstacle if we had just received that unconditional love we so desperately needed in our early development. The space held by an emotionally mature caregiver, a space where we feel safe and seen, gives us the courage to stay present, even when we're scared or hurting.

We were never designed to do this alone, but because we abundantly lack access to emotionally mature humans, we have to be willing to do the work ourselves once we have enough self-awareness to do so. If we can find conscious partners to co-facilitate the process with us without falling into codependency, it certainly helps, but we must at least be willing to do the work on our own. No one else will ever be able to feel our feelings for us.

Love is unconditional; most relationships are not meant to be. Love is a constant energy we can choose to tap into at any time, but relationships are impermanent; they are entered into to serve a particular purpose, based on the conditions of that purpose, and once that purpose is fulfilled, they either change or dissolve.

Healthy relationships among equals are based on agreements of common consent. They are mutually beneficial and avoid abuses of power. Healthy relationships between guardians and their dependents are based on responsibility. The dependent owes their guardian nothing as a natural result of the dependency created in them by the guardian. Without the guardian's consent to be responsible for a dependent, the dependency on them does not exist. Any expectation of reciprocity in a relationship involving the power dynamic of guardian and dependent is an abuse of power that results in domestication.

When all parties within a relationship are equal in ability to influence or leave the relationship, it can result in the kind of external interdependency necessary for a species or society to thrive. When a relationship involves unequal power between the parties involved, and that power is abused, it results in dysfunction, usually in the form of emotional codependency.

For the emotional health of all parties, the only healthy purpose for a relationship between a guardian and their dependent should be one of responsibility toward the care and development of the dependent. As guardians, we are literally protecting and accepting responsibility for the well-being of someone dependent on our care. Once the dependent is emotionally mature, the nature of that relationship would naturally evolve into more equal power dynamics, except where the deliberate creation of permanent dependency is involved. Creating permanent, captive dependency in others, then, such as domesticated animals, is not conducive to, nor motivated by, emotional health.

Everyone starts out as a dependent, and some circumstances result in unexpected permanent dependency, but in general, most beings are intended to mature into full autonomy. Until one has reached an autonomous state, they are not in a position to offer consent to anyone with influence or power over their lives. Dependents do not choose the relationships they are in; they are either created or brought into relationship by those who have authority over them. When one's basic needs are under the control of another, the influence of the one in a position of power negates the possibility of an equal, consenting relationship. Therefore, in order for the relationship to support the best interests and proper development of the dependent, it must be unconditional while dependency exists.

Domesticated animals are permanent, captive dependents created or controlled specifically to be exploited. The nature of their existence goes directly against unconditional love, creating a fundamental flaw in most people's proclaimed love of them. You can feel a wide range of positive emotions while exploiting someone, but you can't love them. To love someone is to be fully present with and for them, without controlling or trying to change them for your own purposes.

To love a dependent is to be in a committed, *unconditionally* loving relationship with them for as long as they remain dependents.

I call this the Guardian Contract. This unconditional relationship is the norm between wild animals and their progeny but rarely consistent in human dynamics. It is nonexistent between humans and domesticated animals (domesticated relationship, not biology), because the nature of domestication negates the unconditional aspect of love.

The nature of pet ownership is symbolic of humanity's disconnect from a deeper understanding of love. One should not have to become a pet in exchange for the love and care we all deserve, but most people do not want the responsibility of being someone's primary caregiver if there is no obvious and direct benefit to doing so. Furthermore, most people don't want the responsibility of leading by example in order to educate the animals in their care, which is why the vast majority of people resort to controlling them through training. The training is only needed in the absence of emotional awareness and authentic leadership, and those are only absent as a result of domestication. Systems of reward and punishment become obsolete under the leadership of an emotionally mature caregiver.

The journey of my own emotional development was sparked from obligation, and if I'm being honest, shame. After experiencing how much the horses in my care evolved once all forms of exploitation had been removed, I felt I owed it to all captive animals to establish the same kind of unconditional relationship I had offered my herd. It began as a righteous sense of duty and quickly turned into a deep dive into understanding trauma, but especially in facing my own. In the absence of exploitation, I suddenly had a lot more time and space to feel it all. To be totally transparent, had I known what an arduous path this was back then, I'm not sure I would have been brave enough to venture forward. There was no book or road map for me, and no one telling me it would be okay. Raw pain and enormous sacrifice lay ahead, and if it weren't for the boundless commitment I feel toward the animals in my care, I might not have survived the process.

Without the Guardian Contract in place between dependents and their primary caregivers, the emotional guidance system becomes heavily distorted. What is being guarded through the contract is the emotionally intelligent connection to Source that supports us in reaching our full power and potential as physically embodied, spiritual beings.

The connection is always diminished through domestication. When domesticating others, we lose sight of love and instead, contribute to a paradigm of codependency masquerading as love. Animal ownership compounds the situation for anyone engaging with it. It is much easier to depend on a captive animal as a source of unconditional love than to overcome the trauma of not receiving or developing it for ourselves. When such dependency exists, and is completely celebrated and normalized by the society one is a part of, the motivation to heal will not be strong enough to move through difficult change until circumstances become dire. Do you feel the direness of the situation yet?

⊙>>>⊙<<<⊙

Chapter 7

INTUITION

Huskies display more wolf-like traits and behaviors than any other breed of dog. They are notorious for being difficult to contain, and they are a common sight at animal shelters. On local social media groups, I regularly read of huskies escaping and just shake my head with humbled knowing.

I am certainly not the first or last person to experience the havoc of these Houdini dogs, but I felt alone on an island of confusion because of what my journey with the horses had exposed. Training animals was no longer an option, and I couldn't see how to bridge what I was doing with the horses to another species, even though my heart knew the work was the same. Why was it so much more difficult with the dogs?

I could always hear my heart beating any time the search was on. Usually, there would be some clue as to which direction she ran in, but mostly I would be driving up and down dirt roads looking for any sign of Denali until she'd suddenly appear. Sometimes, I'd think I would see a ghostly flash of white through the trees, and it would make me change direction. More times than I could call coincidence, those moves would often lead me right to her, though there was no way what I had seen previously could have actually been real. My mind and body started communicating in ways I did not understand, but somehow knew to trust, and it slowly began to get easier to find her.

Once I was more familiar with my local environment, I started looking for Denali on foot whenever she'd take off. It took about six months of living in nature before I finally began to feel part of it. When she would run at that stage, I'd be right behind her, often barefoot. A tuft of hair on sagebrush; a paw print in the dirt; subtle changes in the air I couldn't make sense of—chasing her brought out something primal in me. I had instincts I hadn't consciously felt before, power derived from my own clear perceptions and my legs beneath me.

I experienced exhilaration at levels I had only previously known from the back of a horse or in the arms of a lover, but for the first time, it was coming from and through me alone. As frustrating as it could be to have this feeling associated with anxiously searching for my dog, I loved closing in on the connection to her and bringing her home again and again. Often, she barely had time to enjoy her escape before I was upon her. It started to feel like some twisted game.

The thrill of the chase was always short-lived, though, and never outweighed the burden of responsibility I felt toward keeping her safe. I was heavily torn between overcontrolling her and not knowing how to give her freedom in a responsible way. The game seemed to lose its appeal once Denali figured out I'd be bringing her back home almost as soon as she'd left. This created substantial relief for me, or so I thought. For weeks, the escapes subsided, but in reality, I had merely become hyperaware of her every move as a means to avoid the anxiety that accompanied searching for her. I didn't take my awareness off her. After a while, though, my attention relaxed, and she made her move.

The dogs were unattended outside, and I was in my trailer working, when suddenly, I felt the urge to look out the window. Denali's white tail was swaying to and fro as she trotted nonchalantly toward the road. I threw open the door and said in a stern but calm voice, "Denali. I see you." She stopped and casually looked back at me over her shoulder. I stared back at her. She sighed and slowly turned around to walk over to me. We stared at one another for a few moments, before she sulked back to lie down where I last remembered seeing her. Something was new. Now, not only could I track her effortlessly when she left, my body had also started warning me before she took off.

Of course, I took some comfort in avoiding another wild rendezvous, but the scene had a sickening familiarity to it. I had been able to control the horses with such subtlety as well, and I knew Denali had only listened because she knew I would find her and bring her back. What I really wanted was to keep her from wanting to leave in the first place. Given the stress her escapes caused, I could at least appreciate that some control was better than risking her life, but I knew there was so much more to understand.

What I didn't count on was the cunningness of my dog. Every moment I was spending keeping some of my attention on her, she was doing the very same thing toward me, waiting for her next opportunity to run. It was alarming how even if she could not see me, she somehow knew the exact moment when I became distracted enough for her to slip away undetected; almost as if she could energetically feel our connection weaken just enough to disappear unnoticed. I did notice, though, very quickly. For me, it was as if I could feel the distance between us, and when it became too much, I was on her heels again and trucking her home.

One day I had to leave Denali in someone else's care while I ran errands in town. Taking her with me wasn't an option because every time I tried that, she would just pull the door handle and let herself out of the car the moment I was out of sight. Fortunately, she usually just went looking for me, but I needed to be dog-free to take care of some things. Since I had no way to contain her, I left her harness on, with a 25-foot-long rope attached, and reiterated to the person watching her that she would run if given the opportunity. They must not have believed me. I returned home to find Denali missing, dragging a rope, with fast-fading sunlight and no idea where to start the search.

In the past, I at least had clues about where to pick up the trail to find her. This time, my anxiety was in overdrive, overpowering my instincts. After examining the perimeter of the property and not feeling any hits as to which direction to go, the sun had set before I knew where to begin. When she didn't return after dark, I knew that the rope must have gotten caught on something and that made her vulnerable to the countless coyotes we shared the area with. Overwhelmed by emotion, I shut down, crying myself into an exhaustion-induced sleep. I felt that I had failed her, and that my failure had sealed her fate.

That night, I had a vivid dream, in which Denali guided me to the neighbor's property east of us. I could hear and feel everything that was happening around and inside their home, and I was afraid. I woke up with a jolt just as the sun was offering barely enough light to see. I jumped out of bed, and ran to the neighbor's property. There I found Denali, lying contentedly in the dirt and staring right at me as if she were expecting my arrival. She was indeed stuck, less than a hundred yards from home, her lead tangled up in sagebrush, but completely at ease. Did my dog communicate her whereabouts via the dreamworld? I couldn't know. What I did know is how grateful I was to have found her alive and well. I got rid of that damn rope.

Solutions to my Denali dilemma may have seemed obvious to the average person, but the average person was not going through a major existential crisis, mostly alone in the desert, with nearly 30 animals to care for. The average person was not questioning the entire concept of domestication while also trying to earn cooperation from a powerful animal who valued freedom over everything else. The average person was not exploring the unknown in the most uncomfortable and unfamiliar of ways. I was suffering in the liminal space between knowing what was possible and being where I was at, but mostly, I was overwhelmed and stuck in thinking my work was about horses. As it turns out, it never really had anything to do with them at all.

There came a time when it all finally started to sink in, as far as the dogs were concerned, but not until much later. A friend of mine was visiting and doing some filming, when, while engaged in conversation with her about the horses, my body gave me the warning sign that Denali was about to take off. I looked up just in time to see her moving toward the open wilderness, but this time, instead of calmly addressing her, I yelled out her name in a bit of a panic. She stopped and looked at me like before, but on this occasion, instead of turning around and coming back, she fully considered my "request," then made a mad dash for rugged freedom. My sandals flew off my feet as I took off after her. My emotional experience was caught somewhere between embarrassment, seething anger, and the full-blown bliss of running barefoot and wild, but overall, there was the definite frustration of not understanding why she deliberately ignored me.

The only difference between my first experience catching her about to leave and the next one was how I felt inside. On the day she had listened to me, I had been completely calm. I had been home alone and committed to going after her, so there was no reason to feel any stress. This time, I had guests and was in the middle of something important, and the last thing I wanted to do was be witnessed having to chase down my dog after she clearly demonstrated a complete disregard for my authority.

Ha! As if I had ever had any authority over Denali. When she listened to me, it felt like a fluke, if not a miracle. That changed when I realized she may have been responding to my emotional state more than my words. Of course, that was it. I had been using energy to manipulate horses forever, why on earth would I think it would be any different with dogs? Anything that even remotely resembled manipulation had become cringe-worthy, so the concept simply hadn't crossed my mind.

Manipulating my energy to control my dog was going to be a problem, even if it was in her best interest. I was still way too deep in grieving my former identity as a trainer and master manipulator extraordinaire to even consider using my powers for good. However, I could at least pay attention and see if my energy really was the deciding factor between whether or not she listened to me, assuming I would even be able to control it when the pressure was on. At this stage, it was merely something I was beginning to take notice of.

Between all the time I was spending with Denali, or keeping tabs on her, and experiencing some consistency with her coming to me when asked, I decided it was time to see if we could go on some adventures together. I figured maybe if I got her out a bit, she'd be less inclined to take off on her own from home. The only challenge was going to be how awful it was being dragged by the other end of her leash.

When I used to start horses under saddle and then later go bridleless, there always came that moment where I just had to trust that I had put in the right amount of effort, so that when I swung my leg over their back or took the bridle off their face, nothing bad would happen. The first time I took the leash off Denali felt exactly the same way. Granted, I chose a hiking path that I believed would set us up for success. The trail was narrow, circling around a cinder cone mountain with a pretty steep grade on either side of it. It would not have been terribly easy for her to go off trail, and there was nowhere to go but up ahead of me. I took a deep breath, and unclipped the leash. At first, her excitement propelled her up the trail like a white rocket, but she was barreling back in my direction in no time, and over the course of the next three hours, she stayed fairly close.

The leash was always ready in my hand just in case, but it was similar to the scenario at home where I seemed to be able to more or less keep her close as long as I had my attention on her. In any case, it was a huge step in the right direction, and for the very first time, it was actually enjoyable to go out and do something with Denali. That said, I was making very deliberate choices for risk management, and I was primed and ready to chase her down, which she always knew. It didn't change a thing at home, though, and I was just about at the end of my rope with how to end the endless escapes.

After nearly two years in the desert, a big change finally came. My first book was published, and I purchased a property to start a more formal and public horse sanctuary just over the border in Oregon. We would have a real home again, and it looked like my dream was about to come true.

Of course, Denali had other plans. A big house, plenty of room to run, and tons of visitors to adore her were not enough to curb her solo adventures. Instead, she ran until I began to find in myself what had drawn me to her in the first place. She was always teaching, never really going anywhere; just showing me the way.

Chapter 8
THE HIDDEN COST
OF DOMESTICATION

Domestication is more than controlling another's body. It involves controlling so much of another's inner experience that it literally alters who they are by stifling emotional processes that would otherwise connect them to greater wisdom. There is no such thing as an emotionally mature domesticated animal, including human animals. The very nature of domestication involves overruling someone's natural responses in order to control them or shape them into some lesser, tamer version of themselves. Wild animals are not hard to tame because of their biology; they are hard to tame because they are emotionally aware and able to respond accordingly to threat. No one who knows real freedom would be interested in stealing the freedom of another, and there is a reason that slavery is mostly nonexistent in the wilderness. The wild knows that the true cost of domestication is actually incurred by those who do the domesticating. It is the trading of authentic power for a false sense of control, which is never sustainable long term.

There are multiple ways one individual can exploit another, but from what I can tell, they all lead back to an underlying motivation to feel something other than what needs to be felt. In other words, all forms of exploitation are carried out in order for the one abusing power to either feel something they want to feel or avoid feeling something they do not.

Emotionally aware, mature, autonomous beings do not exploit others, nor can they be easily exploited. They would have no reason or desire to avoid emotion, because the full range of emotions is entirely useful to them. Once we can relate to all emotion as information and process it accordingly, we are invited to step into a space where we can truly be masters of our experience and of creation.

For example, fear, when experienced as a naturally occurring emotion in the body, keeps someone alive. It is not suffering, but rather, a valuable, temporary impulse or instinct to avoid imminent danger. The fear most humans are attempting to avoid through exploitation is psychological, or created from thought, as opposed to the instinctive fear that is necessary for survival. Psychological fear is a very painful, confusing experience because it generates intense emotion from a usually fabricated source of threat. Instead of allowing authentic fear to be a natural guide to keep us out of danger, we create fear from thought that we then try to run away from, further disconnecting ourselves from the truth. This kind of insanity can only be present in one who is no longer wild, and it unfortunately seems to be the most common determinant of human behavior for our time.

Anger is your body's natural call to action to protect and create boundaries, and expressions of anger are likely to be suppressed during the process of domestication. When young animals are not taught healthy expressions of anger, or allowed them, it means that the caregiver has determined that their own conditioned beliefs are more important than the dependent's authentic experience. If expressions of anger are permitted during the process of domestication, a form of abuse, the abuser will then have added challenges in attempting to control the individual they seek to domesticate. This is especially true if the abuser cares about the individual they are domesticating.

I hesitate to use the word "abuse" because of how triggering it is to otherwise kind and caring individuals, but allow me to repeat that domestication only happens through abuse and can only be maintained through such. The simplest definition of abuse is the misuse of something, and all use of anyone is misuse. We have all abused animals; we have all been abused. This is the nature of domestication. It does not make anyone wrong or bad. It is simply the result of our original separation.

One cannot control another being's emotional experience without engaging in an abuse of power, so even when you care a great deal about the individual being controlled, abuse is still occurring in the form of emotionally stunting those you are responsible for.

Training someone to not feel what they are feeling is the first step in disrupting their emotional maturation process and ability to self-regulate. It is also the main source of lingering trauma for just about everyone on the planet. Systems of reward and punishment modify the behavior of young animals without understanding the natural emotions that inform us of our needs. We do not actually have emotional needs. That's a concept based on a domesticated perspective. The only need we have concerning emotions is the need to feel them so we can be informed by them from a place beyond conditioned thought.

Domestication is a vicious cycle. We only domesticate others to tend to the emotional wounds of our own trauma, which is often our own domestication. The dependent in a domesticated relationship is the most obvious victim of the experience, but the real cost, often hidden, is to the one doing the domesticating. When we engage in the domestication of another being, we give up our ability to access our potential. We can achieve a great many things through exploitation. Just take a look around—most human advances have been made at someone else's expense. Exploitation is not sustainable, and the real hidden cost of domestication will only be revealed when it's too late for us to turn things around.

Domestication robs all parties in the relationship of their authentic power and creative potential. Neither side is able to achieve emotional autonomy, nor the fullness of who they are, due to the codependency created within such a relationship. The codependency of domestication then evolves into dependency on external factors for emotional regulation, and this is where it gets even more complex. When someone is easily able to emotionally regulate due to privilege, it becomes nearly impossible to see the harm in domestication.

I have had the great fortune of knowing some exceptional humans, especially in the past decade. Overwhelmingly, these people have had two things in common: first, none of them were heavily involved with animals, and second, they were all very privileged individuals.

Interestingly, those who were able to achieve great outside success as a result of their privilege, but still struggled internally, had pets. Some of the most famous and successful people I know have relied on codependent relationships with animals and other humans to be able to do what they have done. I, too, can relate, as now I fully understand that

I never would have been able to write *Riding on the Power of Others* without the functionally codependent partnership I was in at the time. I'm sure my emotionally enmeshed relationship with my dog Spur contributed a great deal as well. My emotional regulation at that time was still deeply dependent on external support, and I had no idea that was even a thing to be looking at.

The word "privilege" gets thrown around a lot, especially today, but how I am using it here can be defined as "the amount of access someone has to external forms of emotional regulation." Therefore, privilege can be anything as obvious as skin color and the amount of money someone has to how emotionally supported they are in their relationships and everything in between.

Privilege is not good or bad; it just is what it is. Some forms of privilege involve abuses of power, such as pet ownership, and some do not, such as having healthy friendships. What matters here is how much dependency we have on our privilege to do the things we do and behave as who we believe ourselves to be.

There was no way for me to understand how much privilege I had before I began applying this work to dogs. When only focused on horses, I tapped into the core essence of where it all leads and found an anchor there, but everything changed when I shifted my focus to the main animal no one wants to get honest about: "man's best friend."

The result was losing most of my friends, my partner, my home, the support I had for my developing sanctuary, all my money, and my nonprofit. Of course, my own trauma and lack of understanding around emotion and healing contributed, but I was having one hell of a time getting anyone to want to look at what I now believe to be the core wound of our species. A lot of people could get behind not riding horses, especially when they themselves had no emotional attachment to those animals, but not having emotionally enmeshed relationships with dogs? Get outta here! So I did.

I moved back to the desert and found myself mostly alone for a few years with not enough support to care for nearly 30 animals. Somehow we got through, but not without bumps and bruises along the way. To call it "a painful time" is inadequate. I lived in extreme circumstances, caring for many others when I was barely learning how to care deeply for myself, and it broke me—wide open. I thought I had already been broken open, but the layers of privilege are many, and having taught this work to many people over the years now, one thing I can say for certain is that unearned privilege may be the biggest obstacle to overcoming one's own domestication. The more one has, the less likely one is to lean into emotional pain. It is just far too easy to reach for something soothing.

Are you ready to get really uncomfortable? It just gets more painful from here. If you are abundantly resourced, it will require enormous courage to choose pain when you don't have to. However, you're already in some amount of pain or you wouldn't be here, reading these pages. I can tell you from experience that the pain is worth it, and even more so, it becomes a friend once you realize that there is nothing to fear about it. The result is you get to love yourself. Hell, you get to actually like yourself, too. No one can stop you from becoming all you want to be or from living the life you want to live except you. No one.

To be wildly human is to create. We are literally God expressing itself through human form, and the separation from that knowing, that divine experience, is the real hidden cost of domestication. To come here and not create your reality through your own deliberate thoughts, words, and actions is a waste of the miracle of what it is to be human. Your body is the doorway to freedom; your emotions your truest intelligence. That is the greatest gift the animals have to offer us: to remind us beings how to be in our bodies, guided by soul intelligence rather than conditioned beliefs. The only thing that sets us apart from the rest of the animal kingdom is that we get to be magicians with the knowing. Are you ready to access your magic?

◉»>◉«<◉

PART TWO

>>>◉<<<

BE LOVE

Chapter 9

INSPIRATION

The great thing about moving closer to civilization was having more people to help. The awful thing about moving closer to civilization was . . . having more people to help.

On a practical level life got a lot easier, because I was sharing responsibilities with three other capable adults and had modern conveniences like a flushing toilet again. On another, I was surrounded by people who were not fully committed to the work, thus inadvertently thwarting my efforts with the dogs.

At least, that's how it seemed from my perspective. The reality was that I was getting a close-up view of how it didn't matter how much I knew if I wasn't leading by example and embodying the work. I didn't even know what that meant yet. The contrast between the calm, balanced, undomesticated herd of horses and the dysfunctional pack of dogs was stark. I was beginning to understand what made things so much more difficult with the canine crew.

Aside from the fact that my work was largely based on my experiences, specifically, with horses, the most apparent difference was, of course, proximity. Following the guidelines was easier with the horses. They were turned out on the land, and when anyone spent time with them, it was planned, deliberate, and the horses made it easy to remember the rules, since I had already done the work to empower them in their interactions with humans. The dogs, however, were around us constantly, leaving little room for me to manage the exchanges between my new roommates and our combined pack of seven pups.

Something much more challenging was presenting itself, though. It did not matter how well I explained what behaviors to disengage from, there was an addictive quality to our connections with the dogs that simply wasn't as present with the horses. The emotional attachment ran deeper than anything I could have anticipated when choosing this path, and the real value of my work was only beginning to show itself.

Though I hadn't figured out exactly how to take the dogs through the same process I had used to "undomesticate" the herd, I was certain of a few things that had to end. One was the incessant baby-talk that had me about ready to put my head through the wall of our new home. It didn't matter how many times I brought it up or how much the others admired my work and agreed we had all come together to put it into practice, the high-pitched tones and blind condescension were relentless, and it was driving me nuts.

Out in the desert, there wasn't a lot of talking. I was often the only one who spoke English there, but the animals and I were speaking a language older than words, so speech was unnecessary. The people helping me create the new sanctuary didn't remember this language yet, and my frustration wasn't inspiring much change.

Out of nowhere, a confronting concept was emerging as the centerpiece of the work: overcoming codependency. I had not been emotionally dependent on horses since I hit puberty. If anything, I had been emotionally detached from them until Shai came into my life, and the love I had for him, and now the others, was anything but attachment. It was truly unconditional, which is what had inspired the first book. Now, I was uncovering layers that none of us were ready to face. It was a daunting realization to see just how much more difficult this was going to be in relationship to those whose love I depended on to feel okay in the world.

When I gave it more consideration, it seemed impossible for the path not to lead here. Every devastating thing in my life, every rock-bottom pit of despair, and even the very inspiration for the work to come to life had been born from codependency. Even the "love" I derived so much power and confidence from in my previous relationships was codependency. I may have found freedom through and with horses, but when I took a moment to look around at the other areas of my life, I was still very much riding on the power of others.

What a humbling awareness. I knew the soulful place I had touched with the horses was real, but maybe I had only peeled off the top layers. Maybe giving up all use of horses was only dusting off the cover of a truth whose depths I couldn't quite yet fathom.

Denali was not my emotional binky. That job was reserved for Spur, and addressing it with him was beyond comprehension at that stage. Fortunately,

Denali kept me too busy to concern myself much with future grief. I was at least getting out and adventuring more with her, which seemed to lessen her desire to run. She wasn't taking off very often, but now we lived next to a busy road and near town where she could get in a lot more trouble. Four pairs of eyes certainly helped in monitoring Denali's whereabouts, but there were also infinitely more distractions than there had been alone in the desert.

Twice within the first few months of our move, I received calls from kind passersby that had picked her up, up to nine miles from home, before any of us had even realized she had left. The second time should not have happened, but Denali taught herself a new skill I did not see coming.

I was in the yard when I got the call that she had been picked up several miles away, but as I thanked the person and hung up on my way to meet them at the gate, I was perplexed. Denali had been contained inside the house last time I had checked. As I came around the front of the house, approaching the gate, I saw the front door was standing wide open. Instantly, I felt fury towards whomever had been so careless to leave it open, but when I investigated further, there were teeth marks imprinted into the door handle. The unruly white beast now knew how to open house doors, too.

The new house stood between the road and a creek, and on the other side of the creek was a steep embankment that gradually climbed and expanded into the 20-plus acres the horses were turned out on. One morning, I felt that all-too-familiar ping that Denali was making an exit. I rushed outside to see her on my side of the creek, then shouted her name. A feeling of dread overcame me, as thoughts of traffic and embarrassment over her behavior flooded my mind, making the calm that could reel her in completely inaccessible. I swear I saw her smirk right before she leapt the creek and took off up the hillside.

I started running, but I knew I couldn't keep up with her running uphill, through thick trees and brush. The land was not yet familiar to me, and I just remember scrambling over and crashing through whatever was in my way, going as fast as I could possibly go to reach her. Every ounce of me was committed to the chase, no matter how much my lungs began to sting. I had to keep her from reaching the road. Catching up to her seemed far-fetched, but I was at least able to keep her in my sight. Up the hill we went, leaping, dodging, and ducking under branches. Then, down again, as I prayed I was somehow avoiding the abundance of poison oak I noticed sprawling across the landscape for the first time.

As if my heart wasn't already pounding from the physicality of it all, Denali was getting closer to the road now that we were headed downhill and back in that direction. We had made it much farther down the property, far away from the house, where the creek ran parallel to the road with only a short, steep slope between the two. My feet pounded the earth harder than I could ever remember them doing before, as I raced to catch her before she hit the pavement.

When she made it to the water, I took a flying leap off the hill, landing in the middle of the creek, about 30 feet downstream from my insubordinate dog. I could barely breathe. I knew I couldn't keep going, and I was surprised to find Denali looking back at me curiously as I gazed at her with a painful look in my eyes.

In my head I heard *Uggggggggggh!*, followed by the words, *Please, girl, just stop,* and in the next moment, my body went into complete surrender. There was nothing left to give, and no fight left in me. I felt every bit of the emotion I was experiencing, flooding through my body in total nonresistance. I looked at her once more, before turning to trudge out of the creek, defeated.

Suddenly, Denali was at my side, without any effort, calmly walking beside me, all the way home. I said nothing, but I had been here before. This was the same kind of surrender that had brought a similarly wildish stallion to rest his head on my chest a few years earlier, changing my life forever. I finally knew what had to be done. It was time for Denali and I to head back into the wild, and this time, we would go together.

Chapter 10
REWILD YOUR HEART

The balance maintained by the wild has become critically compromised by humanity's denial of our interconnected truth. The only force that can restore this balance lives purely only in that which remains wild. A better word for that force is *love*, but it has absolutely nothing to do with romance or the warm, fuzzy feelings of affection. The truest form of love is interchangeable with words like *presence*, *wild*, and even *God*. Love is a container for expansion that cannot be defined by any lesser part of itself but requires seeing the bigger picture.

The interconnectedness of the wild is ever present in each of us. All that keeps one from accessing it are the various layers of conditioning resulting from our own domestication. No concept in our lives seems to have become more domesticated than love. The love most of us know and crave is easy to package and sell; therefore, it isn't hard to understand how we have lost sight of love's true meaning. Heartbreak is one of the most painful experiences most humans will ever face, so selling the idea that it can be cured through the affection and admiration of another is a lucrative endeavor.

What those that would sell us such false ideas didn't count on, though, was the truth. Wild hearts cannot be broken. When there is nothing to run away from, it's harder to sell false ideas of well-being, and wild beings are harder to control than those who have been taught to believe they are less than whole.

In this chapter, I'm going to help you begin to rewild your heart by sharing what undomesticated animals have taught me about the true nature of love. If you look up the definition of love in the English dictionary, it's pretty vague and tends to center around affection, pleasure, and attachment. For the purposes of this work, this book, and what

I highly recommend for your life, don't trust the dictionary to define love for you. There is great suffering to be found on the other side of that version of love, and real love is defined through the experience of it, where all emotion is welcome as subtle, graceful guidance in discernment, once we mature.

While all of the feelings mentioned above can arise from love, they are only tiny parts of a much vaster whole. True, authentic love is not a feeling or an emotion. Love is an interconnected state of being that feelings and emotions, not just the positive ones, move through. It is pure presence—the fully embodied, present awareness that all beings originate from and the thing that connects us all together still. "I love you" translates into "I am present with you." Love is the one, absolute truth—what remains when all story falls away. True love is always irrevocably wild, and the only thing keeping us from living in it is our trauma. We are naturally present to love, just like wild animals, once trauma is addressed and energy can flow freely again.

We cannot experience wholeness or connection through exploitation. Surface level needs that make us feel whole and connected can certainly get met through the use of others, but those feelings are fleeting and only last as long as we have access to whatever external source they are derived from. In an authentic state of love, we can feel and experience ourselves as the essence that is primary to our individual physical, mental, and emotional lives. Animals that are free of domestication, both nonhuman and otherwise, operate first and foremost from this state and only secondarily as individuals. They relate to one another not first as human, horse, bear, or dog, but as the underlying energy operating those various physical forms. The information that comes through this primary connection is what establishes and maintains harmony and balance among all life on the planet. This is the wisdom of love, and of the wild. This is love.

The first time I experienced true love as a constant was with a horse. It was messy, ugly, and painful. It was also the most intimate experience of my life until that moment, and it changed my course forever. I had been practicing what I thought to be a new relationship-based training method with my stallion Shai—except it wasn't training and it wasn't a method. Without knowing it, what I was practicing was unconditional love in action. By removing all ways of controlling who he was or chose to be, I was left in the discomfort of my own vulnerability with no way of hiding my deepest feelings. Left with no other option, I surrendered to what was happening within.

Experiencing those feelings in a totally embodied way, without a story and without projection, brought us together as one. He literally moved in harmony with what I was experiencing inside myself, and because I had not abused my power over him as his guardian or conditioned him to be subordinate to me in any way, there was no doubt about the authenticity of what had taken place. Shai was a horse that would not hesitate to hurt me if I showed up as anything less than love. When I met him in complete presence, it was like having a conversation in a language neither of us needed to learn. My mind could try to make sense of it after, but while it was happening, my mind wasn't even involved. This was only the beginning.

After Shai helped me find my way back to love, I was very hungry to learn and understand more. I took a serious interest in the state that I very naturally surrendered into when I would spend time with the horses in an unconditional, agenda-less way. I felt completely safe and at ease with the horses, so there was nothing keeping me from feeling whatever came up inside my body. Never had I allowed such raw emotion to move through me, and at that time in my life, I probably felt safer with the horses than I felt with myself or anyone else.

I began to realize just what it was costing animals to live in domesticated states for human use. I realized how domesticated most of us humans had become as well. To experience the fullness of this deeper understanding of love on the other side of the many highs I had previously thought love to be was devastating, to say the least. To this day, I'm not sure there is anything more painful than realizing the love you gave someone you cared for deeply was more about you than them, and even less about love. Real love is unconditional and always present. Real love is never motivated by what you hope to gain through offering it to another.

It took a few more years, but with love's deeper wisdom guiding me, I finally realized why many adult humans and domesticated animals suffer so greatly from the emotional wounds of childhood or other trauma. The love most of us were raised on is hardly the unconditional, present, interconnected love of the wild.

Chapter 11
INITIATION

Watching the sun rise over a mountain landscape is one of my favorite experiences. While the rising sun can hold the hope of a new day no matter where I am, being surrounded by mountains, or better yet, standing on one, imbues that hope with a courage and awe that always inspires me to reach out and meet destiny.

Amid my own distractions, it had taken nearly a year after the move from the desert for me to figure out how to begin transferring what I had learned to the dogs. Denali was the obvious choice for whom to start with, since I clearly had no external influence over her and would have to earn every inch of her cooperation.

Fed up with my own inconsistencies, knowing everything I had sacrificed and suffered would never help people if it were limited only to horses, I made one of the most disciplined decisions of my life. I began getting up at 5 a.m. every morning and taking Denali up a mountain.

In late spring, with snow still on the ground above 5,000 feet, destiny got my feet moving into an important new chapter. The plan was to simply apply everything I had learned with the horses in principle and respond accordingly, trusting that it would work the same way. The challenge, and significant difference, was the parameters. Horses live in contained systems called paddocks or pastures. They don't live at our sides with the option of running off into the unknown. With the horses, applying the principles was simpler in that there was some element of a controlled environment in place. What would love look like when that element of containment was absent?

We would leave the house in the dark, arriving at the trailhead just as the sun would offer pink and purple hues on the horizon. At the base of the trail each morning, I would stop to take in the glorious view, breathing in the summit of Mount McLaughlin in the distance. Nothing has ever felt better than experiencing my ultimate connection in the physical wilderness, grounded right into the earth through my own bare feet. Sharing those moments with Denali rooted me more into being than anything I had previously known, and I felt proud to be taking this step with her.

Until then, our relationship had been mostly burdensome for us both. Denali didn't want to be controlled. I didn't want to control who she was or her life beyond my responsibilities as her guardian. We had different takes on what those responsibilities were, and I was beginning to think she was probably the wiser on the subject.

For years, we lived in this liminal space of possibility, frozen in the land of potential, though I suppose that only describes me, since I had total control of the situation as the one in a position of power. Fortunately, Denali's true self had remained intact because I had refused to train or force her to comply with the domesticated world; however, not knowing what to do instead had put her at great risk and cost me enormously. It was time to change that, without sacrificing who she was.

Step one: Release the beast. As I suspected, Denali took off up the mountain ahead of me and was out of sight within seconds. Anxiety rippled through me, as thoughts of what might happen began taking over my mental chatter. Swallow. Deep breath. Come back to the body. I didn't need to play out every possibility to know the potential risks. I knew them and accepted them. I had chosen this trail because it was remote and we would not have to concern ourselves with other humans for a few hours while I figured things out. I could trust myself. I could trust her to come back. She understood the wild better than I did and was less a threat to it or threatened by it than my own domestication. All I needed was to be here now, in my body and with her. So I started walking, and I kept most of my attention on what I was feeling inside.

The trail was tough at first. Physically, I wasn't in the best shape to be keeping up with a husky on a mountain, but more than that, I was surprised to learn how much fear lived inside me.

"Fearful" wasn't a term used to describe me often, or even once that I could recall. I was known for courage and bravery, not anxiety. I didn't even know I had anxiety before it was revealed on that mountain.

The most disturbing revelation wasn't the fear itself but what I was afraid of. I wasn't worried about bears or mountain lions or what might happen if one of us got hurt. Overwhelmingly, each step up that mountain revealed that it was the opinions of others I worried about the most. I was afraid of being seen as crazy or irresponsible, afraid of not being loved or accepted, but mostly, I was afraid that at a very fundamental level, I was just bad or wrong.

The experience in the creek that inspired this plan was the first time I fully recognized just how much my internal state had been influencing Denali. I knew how to manipulate my emotions to affect the behavior of animals. I had done that for years in my horse training. What had never occurred to me was how much the unprocessed emotions of the past could affect those around me. Wild creatures are very put off by our inability to process our feelings and be present with our surroundings. Denali was one of the wildest not-wild creatures I knew. Inside every domesticated animal, including human animals, is a wild creature desperate to return to this state of emotional awareness and maturity. When you can access it and allow it to communicate with others, that's when real conversations can begin.

In that moment of complete surrender, after the stakes had seemed really high, my desire for her to return home with me was clearly communicated without the static of fear. Denali had less reason to move away from me in the absence of fear, and that's when it hit me. The best way to keep an escape artist home is to create a home they no longer want to escape from. Denali was my permanently captive dependent, which, to a large degree, makes me her home. I had to become the home she no longer wanted to escape from. The only way to do that was for me to become a home I also no longer wanted to escape from. Yikes!

If I wanted to reach Denali, I knew I would have to become like her. So I did. I felt every emotion, dropped every story, used every step toward her as an opportunity to release something trapped inside me that no longer served. As a child, it had never been safe for me to feel my feelings, nor was that modeled or even spoken about. I had built up a great deal of armor and resistance to vulnerability as a means of protecting myself, especially when I was afraid of someone else's reaction or becoming their prey.

Applying this work to dogs, out in the open, was bringing up so much more than what I had experienced in the pastures back at home, and it was becoming clear that the armor would have to come off if I wanted to connect with this dog, just as it does any time I am alone with a horse. The tears I shed on that trail were many, and the emptier I became, the less distance Denali put between us.

Each day on the mountain brought us closer together in every way imaginable. She would remain out of sight for long stretches of time in the beginning. After only two weeks, that changed dramatically, and it would be rare if I lost sight of her at all.

The trust and faith it required to move through those periods were daunting. Every voice would emerge to challenge or question my judgment around what I was attempting and what a horrible dog guardian I might be if something happened to Denali.

There I was, using the wisdom of my extensive knowledge and experience with animals to challenge every societal norm, deep in the wilderness where no one could see to criticize, and somehow I managed to bring every single hater and critic on the trail with me, anyway. These were the very same people still eating animals, riding horses, and using systems of reward or punishment to train the authentic essence right out of the animals they claimed to love, all out there telling me what a terrible person I was for letting my dog run wild where surely the worst was bound to happen.

I started running toward those voices as fast as my feet could carry me. Anger pounded in my chest and down through my strengthening legs, while steam lifted off my cheeks as hot tears met the freezing, mountain air. Denali would suddenly appear from above a rock outcropping and leap down beside me, joining me in stride, running together, a pack of two. The more real I got, the more she wanted to be with me, and the less I cared about what the voices were saying. The more I felt, the less I heard them at all.

The mountain became our sanctuary. How strange to think the dangerous wilderness felt safer than the civilization below, but it was true, and I began to understand more about why Denali ran. The path below our feet and paws may have been there already, but we were rewriting how we moved across it together.

Denali was showing me something profound, and my relationship to animals was at the root of it. Domestication was not who someone was, or their biology, but how they were treated and who they were allowed to be by someone in a position of power over their lives. Domesticating someone was a choice. In each moment, we could choose to love those in our care or choose fear in the form of exploitation. It really was that black or white, even when nothing else is. How in the world would we ever be free if our daily practice was that of controlling, manipulating, or enslaving others, but especially while calling it love?

My heart sank deep in my chest as I considered the implications of what I was discovering on that mountain.

Every single animal lover I knew—even, and maybe especially, those fighting for the rights of other beings—was playing out the same madness on some level. That certainly included me, even while learning to see and change it. I thought about Spur back at home, and how much I still needed his love; how much harder this was going to be to implement with the emotional binky corgi as opposed to the wolf. As long as we believed we had a right to domesticate or create permanent, captive dependency in others, we would all be guilty of playing a role in the disconnect causing so much havoc on our planet. I love this planet and everything wild far too much to remain part of that destruction.

The difficulty was that people did not understand the abuse of power involved with domestication, nor are most of us present enough to recognize all the subtle ways we unnecessarily control others as a means to avoid our own fears. As a society, we certainly don't recognize the costs, and the biggest ones reached far beyond the individual lives affected, even when death occurs.

The worst part about everything that was becoming clear to me? Overwhelmingly, most of the unnecessary control exerted over animals is referred to as "love." My grief was enormous, and I had yet to even learn what it truly means to grieve. Yet again, I was entering terrain on a frontier that would surely isolate me even more from the vast majority of humanity ... and people thought not riding horses was brave. Bravery would be finding a way to create a practical body of work around these concepts, and then, quite literally, unleashing it into the world.

⊙>>>⊙<<<⊙

Chapter 12

UNDOMESTICATE
YOUR LIFE

At the root of all other planetary crises on Earth is an emotional health crisis. We don't have a healthy relationship to or understanding of emotion, and the vast majority of human adults have not reached emotional maturity. Depression, anxiety, addiction, personality disorders—these are all emotional regulation problems, not just mental illness.

The cause is our own domestication, and the problem is perpetuated by our domestication of others. When we undomesticate our lives, we create the space to revere and fully experience life rather than exploit it. Within that space, we have the opportunity to heal and restore connection to that which allows emotion to inform the body as designed.

We are not as broken as we think. We've simply forgotten how to be animals. The bodies we inhabit are divine links to a more interconnected existence that is free of the psychological burden of suffering. When the mind is given more attention than the body, a false story is created around who and what we are. Controlling external factors for a contrived sense of safety or seeking emotional highs is not the answer. We must learn how to feel and process all of it, the way nature intended, if we are to elevate human consciousness out of a paradigm of fear that is threatening our very existence. You are more powerful than you remember. Put your primary focus on restoring access to that which has been buried by your conditioning. Heal what's going on in you and the dependents in your care before worrying about rescuing anyone else or saving the world. When you do, you'll find your way back to the only thing that ever could: undomesticating your own life.

No one is born domesticated . . . not even a French bulldog. We all start out wild, no matter what atrocity had to occur to welcome us into this reality. If you weren't already tapping into your wild again, you wouldn't be reading this. I know a little French bulldog named Philippe. He taught me the value of seeing past our exterior in order to understand the wild within us all. For the first year of his life, it was a real battle between honoring who he really was and judging the package, and cause, of his physicality. Clearly, anyone who thinks wolves domesticated themselves hasn't spent time with a French bulldog. Every day, though, as I observed him growing within the container of this work, there was only one true message being received, and that was how truly joyful he was about being alive. Keep in mind that he was undomesticated right from the start, but his joy, that's somewhere inside each of us, no matter what brought us into earthly existence.

The first step to "undomesticating" your life is to develop enough self-awareness to not only begin noticing the thoughts in your head and from where your current beliefs originate, but to directly challenge their validity. If you have the mettle to do that much, what follows herein is just a natural progression. However, it is very difficult for a deeply domesticated human to recognize their exploitation of others, much less have the emotional resiliency to face it. If we are not willing to look for truth, no matter how painful the information may be, then we are not ready to find it. Once we are willing, it becomes absolutely necessary to disengage from the direct domestication of others if we are to have any hope of fully releasing ourselves from our own.

This work doesn't necessarily begin or end with nonhuman animals, but for those with animals in their direct care, the relationship to them is often one of the biggest distractions that must be faced before one can hope to achieve personal autonomy. Think about it. If you're domesticating someone in your home every single day, what's the likelihood you're going to have a clear picture of yourself or the world beyond domestication while in the midst of it as practice? A lot of people who already believe themselves to be autonomous are simply dependent on their privilege. We don't learn how able we are to emotionally regulate and process internal information until we're pressure tested outside the means of external support. Domesticated animals are an enormous source of that external support.

Working with the animals in our care provides a mirror and container for transformation that is seldom available anywhere else. We have a great deal of control and influence over the lives of animals in captivity, so a simple shift in motivation can provide an interesting opening for growth. Those brave enough to do so can shift from the highly exploitative concept of treating animals like property or as emotional pacifiers and swap domestication for evolution through the alchemy of true, unconditional love. Change on this planet is possible, and it won't happen by prioritizing the symptoms of a domesticated world. Real change starts inside each of our own hearts, on our plates, in our homes, and with our families, including our animal kin.

In our current culture, there is no place other than our homes for animals that cannot survive in the wild if they are not being heavily controlled to fit into a domesticated society. Even the vast majority of animal rescues/sanctuaries utilize all sorts of subtle and not-so-subtle, unnecessary forms of control to keep the animals agreeable and safe for visitors and caretakers to be around, and especially as an emotionally exploited source of funding. It is in our homes, and by consciously signing the guardian contract, that each of us has the opportunity to reveal the truth of our relationships with animals and begin an enormous individual and collective healing process.

Permanently captive animals can only become semiautonomous once all exploitation has ended and they are allowed to heal from the trauma of domestication. Some animals and situations invite more autonomy than others. A horse that is allowed the space and means to live as naturally as possible within a fenced, physical boundary will become far more autonomous than a dog living in an apartment with little access to unrestricted movement and independent choices.

In general, though, the animals in our care will remain dependents, as a result of their captivity and, therefore, our enormous influence over them. This power dynamic is unrecognized among animal lovers, and forms the slippery slope that leads to emotional exploitation.

It is not a child or dependent animal's job to emotionally regulate the very being responsible for teaching and modeling emotional regulation to them. The only loving way to be in relationship to a dependent is to care for them unconditionally. Dependent animals in our care are not our friends. They are our permanently captive dependents, and therefore, our responsibility. We can enjoy enormous mutual benefit from these relationships, but only when our needs are not placed on those in our care.

Domesticated animals are completely dependent upon us for their basic needs. They are not here to heal us or help us or carry our emotional or physical burdens. They are here, quite literally, because we enslaved them and continue to keep them emotionally stunted through our use of them. There are plenty of people out there that would claim that captive dependent animals have agreed to some soul contract that excuses our exploitation of them. I call that spiritual bypassing, and more importantly, domesticated humans have no clue how to interpret soul essence agreements before they've undomesticated their own lives.

So much of what we think we know about animals has been interpreted and decided upon through a domesticated lens. Even trusted science becomes unreliable once we realize just how much of it has been determined through exploitation, and for exploitation, as opposed to deeper truth. Domestication actually keeps us from discovering the science we're capable of accessing for broader understanding.

My experience applying this work with horses, for instance, proved nearly everything I was taught about equine science in college to be largely incorrect and entirely limited in perspective. One thing about this work I've found to be consistent since day one is that the results are demonstrably and objectively repeatable, without fail, no matter what animal they are applied to, and I trust that as science far more than any textbook written by someone who has no experience with animals outside of controlling them.

Having animals does not mean we must use them. On the contrary, we are responsible for those we create or bring into our lives that are unable to care for themselves. By choosing to love those in our care unconditionally, not only do we give them the freedom and well-being of emotional autonomy but we also get a chance to live the life we were made for by discovering the power we have within us to shape our reality and consciously evolve. It is only through unconditional love that we achieve emotional maturity, and therefore, the ability to stay constantly, reliably connected to our own soul's guidance to reach our greatest potential. The greatest outcome? Eliminating unnecessary fear from our lives, which leads to the end of all suffering.

Chapter 13
INCUBATION

Weeks floated by, and things were changing, dramatically. Denali was changing, I was changing, and our relationship actually deserved to be called that, finally. The first, huge, noticeable change was gifted to me by a large, beautiful doe. Denali was a short jaunt ahead of me on the trail when I first saw the deer moving speedily across our path. Anxiety leapt up inside of me with the thought, "Oh, no, she's going to chase the deer and prove I'm completely nuts and making all of this up." I just knew Denali wouldn't be able to contain herself and stay with me instead of chasing a deer.

As I came around a sharp curve behind them, a tree made me lose sight of both for a split second, and I fully expected to be on the chase as soon as I rounded the corner. To my surprise, the deer was bounding off into the distance but Denali had stopped and turned around to wait for me.

Maybe you would have to have experienced the many miles I've run after my dog while she runs after a prey animal, but I became overwhelmed with emotion. That was the first time in our history when it was blatantly obvious that Denali had chosen me over her own instinctual nature. To be more worthy of her attention than a wild animal on the run seemed like a pretty big deal to me, and I communicated it gratefully as she wagged her tail and licked the tears off my face. Observing her in awe, day after day, I realized that we can never fully know anyone else. Not if we love them. I saw with such clarity that Denali was constantly growing and evolving, as a being in her own right, just as I am. My greatest honor in love was simply to bear witness to her becoming.

Every time I tried to limit her in some way, or say I knew who she was, or tell people about her, or try to describe her personality, every time, she'd remind me how little I knew by gracing me with a new version of herself out on that trail. It was always a more vast, more amazing, more free version of her that I did not even know she was capable of. Witnessing her unstoppable evolution inspired me and gave me great hope that each one of us has that same ability to be constantly growing and moving toward something more real. I don't know why anyone wouldn't want that. Yes, it's scary and challenging at times, but at the end of the day, if you just remove yourself from the people who tell you what is and isn't possible, saving your considerations for those who are actually in the arena with you, there is so much wisdom the natural world has to offer. And fortunately, the natural world exists right there in our very own homes, even in captivity, if we will just learn to allow ourselves and others to be what it really means to be free.

Life has a funny way of offering up what we need, even when it isn't what we think we really want. Less than a year after I became fully committed to transforming my relationship with Denali, our circumstances changed and we no longer had easy access to our sacred mountain trail. By then, we had gone on many new adventures, but most of them were out in the wilderness and off leash. The work I was doing fully embraced the presence of a leash when necessary by law or for immediate safety, but we hadn't tested those parameters yet. I had taken an office downtown and had Denali with me one afternoon when we were invited to lunch. The anxiety crept back in. What if she's horrible on the leash and makes me look like a fool? And even worse, What if I find out this is all the distorted projection of the mad woman I clearly am? Deep breath, several of them.

For such a mundane excursion to grab a bite to eat, I remember that afternoon as if it were today. I clipped the leash to Denali's harness and prepared myself for the likelihood that I'd have to keep my arm strong to hold her back. As we exited and rounded the corner of the building, to my great relief and astonishment, Denali was calmly and gently striding beside me, even looking up at me in a seemingly reassuring way. We set out for the half-mile walk to the restaurant, and I was nervous because the downtown area is always crowded with people. There I was, writing a book on how choosing love could transform relationships and transcend the need for training, and I had somehow neglected to test that theory in public. I knew in my heart I had nothing to worry about, but the fear of failure, or insanity, was very much alive in the moment the pressure test was underway. I didn't want to let down any of the people I had already assured about the value of this for dogs living by city rules in city homes and every other situation imaginable.

Denali did not pull once. I completely forgot about my human company, in awe of the magical creature before me, behaving like a perfectly trained pooch without a single on-leash practice session and who before, seemed to think leashes were human towing devices. Everyone we encountered on the street or sidewalk stopped to say hello to the stunning white dog with blue eyes. Her paws remained planted on the ground, her demeanor calm and polite. She engaged with everyone she met with manners I myself don't often have, nor could I claim responsibility for in my entire history of caring for dogs. I could barely respond to the strangers as I watched in slight disbelief at just how incredibly polite my dear Denali had become as a result of me allowing her to be authentically wild. Obviously, there was more to it than that, but the irony of the situation was not lost.

As I took a seat at one of the outdoor tables just outside the restaurant, with pedestrian traffic coming from multiple directions, I was again shocked when Denali gently and easily laid down beside me on my first request. I do mean request, as in, "Would you mind lying here next to me while we eat?" because the time for training commands was long over in our little world, as if she ever responded to them in the first place. Lunch was a breeze, and I felt the sweet relief of true cooperation. Never had I experienced such a scenario with a dog before without the use of training or some other form of manipulation.

There is a slightly twisted sense of pride when you have trained an animal to do exactly what you say, even though it only happens through an imbalance of power, but it feels humbling and wonderful to have an animal willingly comply out of simple trust and respect. The goosebumps were real as I looked down at Denali with a heart full of gratitude for her and all she had helped me come to understand. I saw, and actually felt, a young woman approaching from up the block, her eyes looking past me and locked onto Denali's icy blues every step of the way. She stopped and spoke to Denali like an equal, in exactly the same manner I would have coached her had she been a client. Denali calmly wagged her tail in response, and the woman then spoke to me with a depth of intimacy uncommon between strangers before she took my contact information and disappeared. I just looked back at Denali and knew: This is how life is supposed to work.

And then came the fall.

As my understanding of the work deepened, my ideas around sanctuary were evolving more rapidly than our actual sanctuary could handle, and it wasn't long before everything fell apart. My team wasn't ready or willing to take things this far, and I wasn't ready to lead them there. Everyone went their separate ways, and in an incredibly short span of time, I became homeless, broke, divorced, and solely responsible for around 30 animals. To say it was one of the most difficult years of my life would be far more than an understatement, especially after such a burst of success after writing my first book. I moved the horses back to the desert, to a piece of land that had been calling me since arriving from Texas four years earlier. Until I was able to rejoin the herd full time, I spent the duration of our transition back to off-grid life at a friend's mountain cabin with the pack.

Those few weeks were bittersweet in so many ways, but one of the joys of that time was taking the pack on the mountain trails near the cabin. It was like Denali and I were getting to let the rest of the dogs in on our secret, and it was so much fun. That is, it was fun until I began to notice a stark and uncomfortable contrast between my beloved, very domesticated Spur and my dear, undomesticated Denali.

Spur had been with me through it all. He was born into the beginning of my long-time love affair with my first female partner. He bore witness to the shift from being a horse trainer to horse lover, from one side to the other. He traveled thousands of miles with me while I worked, burying countless hoof trimmings in countless barns and pastures after he'd had his fill. He'd seen the ocean and summitted mountains and been through Yellowstone and camped with me in Montana. He was loyal and perfect and true, and my dependence on him to be so was taking its toll on him.

On one of our last pack walks at the mountain cabin, I remember being somewhere in the middle between the six dogs on the trail with me. Denali was at the lead, of course, confidently moving forward on her own while checking back every now and then just to make sure everyone was still together. Spur was at the back, desperately trying to keep up with me despite his poor hips saying otherwise. I heard him whimper very softly, and I looked back and saw the stress in his eyes.

His body was saying No, but he didn't know how to. He needed to be with me because he knew I needed him. But the truth was, I didn't anymore, and I had no idea how to embrace that or let him know. I knew it would look similar to what I had gone through with Denali, but it was going to hurt so much worse because of how much I had needed him in the past to get through so much in my life.

I stopped and looked at him gently. Then I turned and looked up at Denali. She knew how to take care of herself, make her needs her first priority, while still being in relationship to me. He was willing to sacrifice everything for me. Which one was love? The answer wasn't easy, and it certainly wasn't what any human had taught me, but I knew in that moment what love would do for him. I let every ounce of my affection for him fill my lungs, and as I breathed out, the words, "It's okay, boy, you can take care of yourself and stay behind," rolled softly off my lips.

He stopped and looked into my eyes with hesitation before he sighed deeply, relaxed his body, and turned back home. He was sleeping peacefully when we returned from our hike. It was the first time I had consciously put my love for him above my need for him, and my heart began breaking for what I knew was to come.

The last time I had landed in the high desert, I thought I had come unraveled. To some extent, it was true. A massive amount of growth and change occurred, and I wrote a book that many found valuable as a result. The truth is, I had barely scratched the surface and hadn't a clue what unraveling really was. At the end of *Riding on the Power of Others*, it was like I had taken off a single layer of outerwear compared to the nakedness that was about to hit me in the middle of a snowstorm.

About two months after reuniting with the horses at the base of Mount Shasta, the unfathomable happened. I no longer had to worry much about Denali disappearing, so I wasn't hypervigilant about keeping an eye on her.

The morning started out normally, until two humans, myself included, got into a heated discussion fueled by unhealed trauma on both sides. Denali doesn't have a lot of patience for human ego bullshit, so she moved away from the negativity of it all, unfortunately making her way out the open front gate, sniffing around on the quiet country road along our fence line. By the time I came back to reality, she was gone.

I immediately jumped into action to track her down, but it only took a few minutes for my intuition to tell me she wasn't there. Panic set in as I knew what that loss of connection with her likely meant. Engrossed in a massive slip in consciousness, I did not notice the truck pull up and pluck her from less than a hundred yards from where I was standing, my back turned and all triggers engaged in a ridiculous, regrettable argument over what, I do not even remember.

⊙≫⊗≪⊙

Chapter 14
SANCTUARY13

We cannot begin to know ourselves or one another through the mind or through the filtered perception of our individual realities. True knowing occurs through a present state of awareness, without attachment to interpretation. Before I met Shai, I had never really considered how to know another; how to truly love them. He helped break me open, but it was Denali who taught me the rest. Denali helped me understand that Sanctuary13 was not a physical location, not a place, but the lived principles of sanctuary within, and therefore, sanctuary in relationship to others. That is what I most aspire to be—a sanctuary to myself and to all those I choose to love; maybe, eventually, to everyone I encounter.

Before I try to explain more about what Sanctuary13 is, I can tell you what it is not. Sanctuary13 is not the "right" way. It is not the only way. The principles are not rules or dogma. They are simply the pieces I have consistently found present in every encounter with unconditional love. When I place myself in every experience I have had in that expanded state of awareness and understanding, these are the essential elements those moments are composed of, every time. I didn't have this particular roadmap or set of guidelines to follow myself, but my hope was to create a path for those who could use one, potentially avoiding some unnecessary suffering along the way.

No matter the relationship or circumstance, I have found these principles to be reliable, varying only in degree and practical application, depending on power dynamics and the situation. In other words, they are rock solid in their ability to guide you back to truth, no matter what, every single time. They are not *the* truth, only the remover of all obstacles to experiencing it. They are completely free of domestication, providing a clear channel to see, to become aware, to experience what is actually occurring rather than interpreting it through the lens of conditioning. The principles of Sanctuary13 eliminate all the subtle and not-so-subtle distractions that blur our perception. They return us to, and keep us in, a wild, feeling frame of understanding.

One could argue that it makes little sense to create such a heady, concept-based body of work to go beyond concept, and I would not disagree. No one needs Sanctuary13. At the end of the day, all any of us really needs is to learn how to get out of our heads and stay in our bodies in order to feel and process all emotion. However, there is a lot of mental programming and habits of behavior that must be overcome for most of us to be able to get there, and Sanctuary13 is a deprogramming of sorts to clear the space.

Practically applied in relationship to those we have power over, it is reverse training, or what I call "undomestication." Relating to others within the framework of the principles allows us and those we love to reclaim our authentic voices and return to who we were meant to be. Offering this level of relationship to another person is the most precious gift one could ever hope to convey. It is true, unconditional love and acceptance.

Believe it or not, when I sat down in the pasture with the horses one day to figure out what elements were most important in teaching people how to access the deepest states of connection, I ended up with 13. Anyone who knows me knows that is my favorite, if not the most significant number in my life, but I didn't plan it for this. They just rolled out that way.

Thirteen is the number of the Death card in tarot, and without attachment to it being so, I can assure you that if you skillfully apply these principles, everything you think you know about love and relationship will die, and a whole new reality will emerge in its place. That scares the crap out of a lot of people, and I get it. A lot of things in our lives might have to change in the face of deep truth, and none of that is comfortable, but with practice and a deep understanding of this work, we can find grace amid even the most tumultuous change.

As far as practical application goes, Sanctuary13 only works when all 13 principles are applied simultaneously. The principles are mutually inclusive, though each one also stands powerfully alone; however, picking and choosing which ones you want to engage with won't lead you to love, only more distraction and avoidance. My recommendation is to learn each one and embrace it fully as having the potential to lead you to what's possible. You do not have to agree with them right away, but it is imperative that you give them a chance to prove themselves through experience.

Many people have resisted this work without applying it with any sort of conviction. I like to tell people that it's like arguing about the taste of orange juice without ever having a sip. Have the courage to really go for it and then tell me how it does or doesn't work. Chances are, you'll be too beautifully lost in your own connections to bring that discussion back to me.

It takes time to rewire our conditioned thoughts and patterns of behavior, so give yourself time. I changed my entire life by showing up fully present for my horse for just ten minutes a day. That daily practice filtered into everything else I did, expanding into my relationships with the other horses, the dogs and other animals, and eventually my relationship to myself and other humans and even situations. I still have to practice, every day. I still fall into old patterns every day. And every day, I know how to return home to love and stabilize and stay, no matter what comes up in an interaction.

Practice, practice, practice. It will become your compass, but you have to show up for it. No one knows what it looks like ahead of time. I often get asked for more specific instruction, but there is none. Sanctuary13 is the container. Stay within it, and the rest will be revealed. It takes courage. Show up for what's been waiting for you all this time. Trust that the part of you that is most you, no matter how dormant, will arise and know exactly what to do if you're following the principles.

I started with only three principles:

- First, do no harm.

- The horse is always right.

- The horse is an exact science.

These are the three pillars of Nevzorov Haute Ecole, the esoteric school of horsemanship where this path began to unfold for me. For whatever reason, most likely because of how much horse experience I had, combined with how much I had studied psychology and spirituality, these were enough to take me quite far. Along the way, though, I realized there was so much more to understand around power dynamics, trauma, and emotion. Sanctuary13 was born from a deeper, more yin element of connection, as well as a visceral understanding of the pain from experiencing various levels of codependency as love.

Within these principles, you'll find every obstacle covered, especially the ones that pop up most frequently in domesticated and transactional relationships; however, the nuance and layers to their depth and meaning seem never-ending. Sanctuary13 is my personal practice, and my understanding of the principles is in constant evolution through that practice.

Just start where you are with them, and practice to the best of your ability. Regardless of experience, when all 13 are applied with heart, you will have direct access to the kind of truth only love can provide. As your energetic awareness increases through practice, so will the depth of your understanding and application.

To get started, familiarize yourself with the principles in the following pages and make sure you're ready to commit to giving this work a real chance to reveal itself to you. If you feel a strong resistance, it makes sense to put the book down after this chapter. If they inspire you toward possibility, keep going. There is no halfway, if you want to experience what this is.

These principles clear the channels for an entirely different paradigm to emerge, and leaving out any one of them will create barriers to participating in what love has waiting for you. The risk of creating dangerous situations with the animals in your care will also become a possibility if you try to half-ass your way through this work; you must be fully committed to no longer exploiting them. Once you understand the principles and have committed to the process, all it takes is ten minutes a day to lay a foundation for transformation. Commit to showing up in relationship to another being (or your own body) for at least ten minutes each day, practicing all 13 principles simultaneously, to the best of your ability. Start where you're at. That is always enough. With time, as your experiences guide you into deeper wisdom and understanding, your practice will begin extending into your daily life in unimaginable ways.

Each principle begins with a practical level of application to undomesticate patterns of conditioned behavior. This helps break the cycle of relating to others on autopilot and creates space for new possibilities to arise. In the breakdown of the work in this chapter, I will explain the surface application of each principle and also share a deeper, more energetic side to each principle. In ancient Hermetic thought, this is known as "As above, so below," the concept of microcosm and macrocosm, the understanding that smaller systems, such as the human body, are miniature versions of the larger universe.

In my experience, students tend to gravitate toward the principles they are more comfortable with and forget some of the rest. That's not how this works. Sanctuary13 only produces the intended result when all 13 are applied, as I noted above. The order and number of the principles are fairly arbitrary, but having taught this for a few years, I've found that there is a particular order that seems to be more digestible as people are learning for the first time.

Many of your questions will be answered as I discuss the sequence of the principles in the chapter, and the rest of the answers are found in the actual application. Abandon what you've been taught so you can receive the wisdom of your soul. Your individual practice, or choosing to participate in some of my additional offerings outside of this book, will be all you need to expand your understanding as you go.

Obviously, the practical application of each principle will vary slightly with each individual relationship, species, circumstance, and situation. Feel free to reach out if you desire more specific support outside of your practice, but trust that your inner wisdom and the animal(s) you're relating to are more than enough to guide you. An entire book could easily be written for each principle, especially when we look at the differences between how it might look with a caged mouse versus a horse, but let that book be written within you through practice. For those who have no captive, dependent animal to practice with, remember this: The body and mind with which your soul is integrated together make up the most important animal you will ever have to be in relationship to.

One last thing before you begin: Moral judgment is a product of domestication, designed to control behavior through fear. Wild animals trust intrinsic guidance, not a belief system based on good and evil, right and wrong, and the promise of eternal damnation if you do something "bad." Your soul will never lead you to cause unnecessary harm to self or others.

Try your best to stay in the land of cause and effect and away from judgment, or guilt and shame will overtake you at every opportunity you allow those stories of right and wrong to consume you. Accountability, not judgment, is the doorway to truth, and self-compassion is required to succeed at this work. Read on to learn the basic components of each principle, including some examples of their practical application in relationship to captive, dependent animals.

First, Do No Harm

As Above

The first principle, in name, is carried over from my experience with Nevzorov Haute Ecole. On the surface, this principle is about acknowledging the inherent harm caused in relationships built upon abuses of power, which of course includes every domesticated relationship, or relationship to domesticated animals. In order to move forward from here, one must commit to doing one's best to eliminate any behavior or practice that knowingly causes physical or psychological harm to those in our care.

This is a big shift away from much of our common relationship practices with animals, and, as with any of the work that follows, requires a real desire to radically transform one's life beyond "doing the right thing."

I am defining "harm" here as deliberately inflicted injury. Some injuries take time to discover, so just start where you're at with your own good sense. There will certainly be times as a caregiver when certain, deliberate harm becomes unavoidable. It is up to you to cultivate the discernment through your practice around when those times are actually necessary and when they are simply a choice made to avoid getting uncomfortable in the search for better solutions. Domesticating others is easy; loving them is not.

Examples of obvious harm that must be challenged and eliminated include striking an animal in any attempt to control them or defend oneself outside of the most extreme circumstances, using pain or the threat of pain to modify behavior, neglect and/or abandonment, using a captive dependent's body for personal fulfillment (such as riding a horse). Those may or may not seem obvious, but I've yet to meet someone with animals in their care not engaged in any one of them on some level, almost daily.

Remember, you're not making a promise to change everything overnight or even forever. You're giving yourself an opportunity to discover something infinitely more fulfilling than what you're stepping away from by stepping away from it long enough to do the work and find out what's possible. You can always go back to what you were doing; that said, I've yet to see someone do so who actually discovers what's waiting for them on the other side of exploitation.

The key to understanding the practical application of this principle is to "stay golden," meaning follow the Golden Rule: If you wouldn't want to be treated in exactly the same manner, find another way. And remember, you cannot avoid harming others if you are not also fully committed to not harming yourself. Some people really believe they deserve to be harmed, and that is a layer of conditioning that really needs to be pulled back before one can expect to get very far with this work.

So Below

The deeper practice of this principle is all about intention and motivation, as in, what's driving your thoughts/words/actions? The first principle is asking you to literally, first, take a pause, and tune into what is behind whatever you're about to do next. Until you are able to respond more than react, this will actually be a reflection until you have developed enough awareness and self-control to create that pause. In the simplest of terms, everything we think/say/do is motivated by fear or love, contraction or expansion. The difference between them is felt as sensation in the body: Fear has an unstable vibration to it—it's shaky; love is calm and secure.

Choices made from fear tend to result in unnecessary harm, especially in the long term; because domestication in and of itself is derived from fear, a great many of the behaviors we choose within that container are also fear-based. This pause is our opportunity to develop awareness and choose internal over external control, to which animals respond much faster, anyway. They are far more attuned to our energy, which we are often unaware of, than the nonsense in our minds making decisions around how we need to control them. Take note: No animal enjoys being near the vibration of fear unless it's a predator about to have a meal.

Practical Examples

- Never use pain to reinforce/modify behavior (no shock equipment, prong/choke collars, striking, using physical corrections, knotted rope halters, and so on).

- Never give an animal a reason to be afraid of you.

- Make sure the animal's basic needs are always met through your care (nutritionally balanced food, shelter, enough room to move in every way their body is designed, and so forth).

Control Only What Is Yours to Control

As Above

Now things begin to get tough. The foundational element of this principle is to replace unnecessary control with authentic leadership. The reason that is difficult is because most humans are not emotionally mature enough to lead an animal effectively without external control or manipulation. This principle includes the complete elimination of all forms of methodized training, no matter how positive one thinks training can be. Training is reserved for those who have not developed enough inner capacity to simply request and then, through the genuine respect they've earned as a guardian/leader, gain cooperation.

When it comes to the captive, nonhuman animals in our care, who we claim to love, the only thing we have the right to control is how we fulfill their basic needs and the responsibilities involved in managing life with them in it. Controlling who they are and how they behave only makes sense when our desire to use them is greater than our desire to love and care for them. Remember, domestication is not born from love, so this is a radical move away from that to not only restore each being's right to emotional autonomy but to balance on the planet. It takes a truly courageous heart to commit to this process.

Under no circumstances is this principle about throwing responsibility out the window and letting the animals in your care do absolutely anything they want. You are responsible for their safety and well-being, for following the local rules and laws of the land, and for not putting anyone else at risk in your community. You are also responsible for making decisions for your family, which includes your animal kin. The elimination of training will definitely create a challenging liminal space to navigate between training mindset/practice and authentic leadership. It will take time for you to become the leader you need to be to get your animals (or kids) to listen to you without control. Your best helper through that process will be to use neutral, physical boundaries.

Such boundaries create a safe container for your captive dependents to operate within until an emotionally healthy relationship is created between you. For example, a leash is a neutral, physical boundary when it is simply in place to keep the animal from leaving but never used to pull or direct the animal. As you can imagine, this requires enormous patience until the relationship is developed enough that the animal wants to be with you more than any outside distraction. Treats or positive reinforcement might seem like an easy solution to this, but just wait, we will soon be eliminating all of that as well. A complete commitment to no unnecessary control, including manipulation, is required to undomesticate your life and the lives of those in your care.

So, how do we define "unnecessary" in this equation? Basically, if the control you apply is not absolutely necessary for the *immediate* safety and well-being of the animal, it likely needs to be thrown out. That covers an enormous number of daily interactions for most people, so it's a good thing you're not going to try to change everything overnight or shame yourself into new behavior, right? Right.

You are responsible for making sure your animal gets the care it needs. You are also responsible for how, when, and why that happens. As you practice and learn new skills around this work, your discernment will increase to be able to make those decisions with more and more confidence. You will, however, come up against many situations where "necessary" will newly be in question. Much of what we do to control animals is not only unnecessary, and often harmful, but keeping us from living in alignment with who we actually want to be and having the emotional intelligence we deserve.

So Below

What is always yours to control is you—your thoughts, your words, your actions, and maybe most importantly, where you are placing your attention. No one else is your business, not even your dependents. Your dependents' needs are your responsibility, as long as they are dependents, but who they are is their own business. Loving someone is about supporting their unique, individual nature, not shaping them to be something for you or to make your life easier.

In my experience, animal people, and especially horse people, are often addicted to external control. When someone needs a lot of external control in their environment, it signifies that they do not know how to process their emotions and, therefore, make very little effort to control their internal reality. More internal control equals less need or desire to control things outside oneself. When we have enough awareness and maturity to be the one directing our own thoughts, words, behavior, and attention, we become capable of navigating reality as a point of attraction for what we actually desire rather than what we are afraid of. That is a very powerful place to live, and it is also one of the biggest reasons to do this very challenging work.

Practical Examples

- Never use a tool (such as a leash or lead rope) to physically pull/direct the animal. Instead, calm your insides, and request the direction you wish to go, or let the animal lead. In circumstances where time management is an issue, proper planning is a must, and in extreme circumstances, your body can be the neutral, physical boundary as long as you feel neutral inside (if you need to carry someone, for example).

- Replace all previously conditioned training commands with authentic speech/requests, but check in with why you're asking for something, and make sure it's appropriate.

- If an animal jumps on a piece of furniture they are not allowed on (yes, that is your decision to make, but be willing to question its validity), calmly ask them to remove themselves. If you are calm inside, they will most likely comply; however, if that isn't possible, then physically remove them as gently as possible without punishment of any kind.

Expect Nothing

As Above

Dependents in our care owe us absolutely nothing. They did not choose their dependency, and are in no position to offer consent in relationships with substantial imbalances of power. You cannot gain the consent of a captive, dependent animal. They cannot give it. They can say Yes and No to a wide variety of things, but they cannot agree to meet our perceived needs from any sort of mature or equal place.

A common error made by those who desire a better relationship with animals is to "treat them like equals," but the problem there is that captive dependents can never be "equal" in the relationship with their primary guardian, or any human for that matter. They cannot truly be our friends or our partners, our healers, or our teachers because in their worldly forms/psyches, they are not in a position to make those agreements. We can surely enjoy our relationships with them, receive appropriate offerings from them, and certainly learn from them, but ultimately, as a result of their captive dependency, they are first and foremost our responsibility.

It is paramount that we understand and accept the above if we are to step out of our own domestication. Most of us were raised with expectations from our parents, meaning that we lacked exactly the unconditional love and support necessary to fully mature emotionally and be free of trauma. Perpetuating those expectations with those in our care not only keeps the cycle alive but keeps us from evolving beyond them ourselves. A lot of grief can arise when practicing this work, and especially this principle. When we suddenly find ourselves responsible for someone else's needs without expecting a return on that investment, it can be very challenging to step into accountability and accept that responsibility unconditionally. In order to grow, we must do so.

So Below

Expectation, or being attached to a particular outcome or agenda, exudes a specific energy—an energy that most animals want to move away from as quickly as possible. It is a predatory sensation, the sense of being asked to fulfill others' wants without your offering to do so. If you've ever felt an unwanted advance from someone, or pressure to do something you have no desire or obligation to do, then you know the feeling. We project this feeling onto animals regularly, often training them into a state of learned helplessness, but when they are allowed their voice, they will move away from that energy every time.

Beyond learning to not want or expect anything from the animals in your care, learning how to control expectation within your body can pay off by encouraging cooperation in the moments when you do need to lead or relate to the animals in meaningful ways. Expecting nothing is about dropping the attachment to a specific result or the anxiety around not getting what you want. The less you need from them, the more likely they are to offer it, but you shouldn't be asking them for anything that is in service to you rather than them.

Practical Examples

- If your dog is off leash and needs to come closer for safety reasons, ask them to return from a calm state of presence rather than a fearfully attached place of need.

- When trimming hooves/toe nails, engage in the task without attachment to getting it done. This will usually result in less resistance from the animal. They cooperate when they feel safe with you, not when you are attached to results.

- Stop asking animals to serve your emotional or practical needs; in other words, no asking them for comfort. Instead, feel your feelings, and try asking for comfort from a consenting equal.

Love Is Not a Transaction

As Above

This is another tough one. The foundational element for this principle is the elimination of systems of reward and punishment, most especially in the form of treats, including all other types of positive reinforcement. Our job, as their guardians, is to reinforce who they are, not who we want them to be. Using basic needs such as food and acceptance as leverage to control behavior is a gross and often completely overlooked abuse of power that has catastrophic results in terms of emotional development. Food and being seen, and acknowledged as good enough just as we are from our primary caregivers, is something that should be guaranteed, not something to be earned.

The difficulty in this principle is recognizing how often the relationship has been built upon the transaction rather than an authentic connection. If an animal only listens to you or wants to be with you when offered food, affection, or praise, then the relationship has very little integrity, and that can bring on all sorts of difficult emotions to sort through. However, that's exactly what this work is for: to create the space to learn how to process emotion, and thrive as a result of having done so.

Too much of the "love" people want and feel is actually what they are getting from or giving to someone else, rather than the deep sense of well-being that arises from real love. Give to your dependents unconditionally, so they can experience that deeper love for themselves, and as a result, you'll earn their respect and desire to be with you without the need to bribe them for it.

So Below

Energetically, trust cannot be bought. The animals in your care are keenly aware of what is absent in you when you feel it necessary to offer something outside of yourself to earn their cooperation. They don't trust you when you offer them a reward; they trust the consistency of the reward. The reward actually creates an enormous obstacle to forming an authentic relationship, in that it eliminates the truthful building of trust. Trust is earned through emotional congruence and consistency of behavior. We only ever need to leverage food, affection, and praise in the absence of being totally trustworthy. When you feel safe to be around, because your internal experience matches your external behavior, you simply won't need to manipulate those in your care. Your influence over them is already huge. Just show up as someone worthy of being followed. What makes you trust and respect someone? The animals in your care probably feel similarly, even if more finely attuned.

Practical Examples

- Replace "Good boy/girl" with an authentic "Thank you" for appropriately requested behavior (such as returning home, not for any sort of performance).

- Offer food and treats freely and unconditionally, in an unattached manner, but never in exchange for desired behavior. Dependent animals do not need to earn their basic needs.

- Do not make an animal take a treat from you for the sake of getting to experience a fleeting moment of closeness with them. Asking them to come to you to receive the treat is still leveraging food for something. This is often the first step in taking the wild out of an animal.

Speak Only with Reverence

As Above

Welcome to what may be the hardest habit to break—at least it was, and continues to be, for me. This principle primarily involves the complete elimination of "baby talk," or any type of condescending or disrespectful speech toward those in our care. Everyone does it on some level or another, and it is often one of the most difficult patterns of behavior to change, because it is rarely questioned and has such an immediate emotional payoff.

Our influence over captive dependent animals is enormous. Just changing our tone can influence them into a different emotional state, which we may be unconsciously controlling to elevate our own.

For example, everyone loves to be welcomed home by a dog that's happy to see them, but what if that "happiness" is actually emotionally enmeshed attachment on display, simply because the dog can't regulate themselves enough to avoid reflecting their guardian's excitement? Thus, on the days when the guardian isn't in the mood, the dog's excited behavior, which has been conditioned, might even be punished for being annoying. There are countless examples of how humans manipulate tone and language to get a desired emotional response from an animal in their care, but the real harm lies in the way it leads to dysregulation all around.

Being unaware of how we are directing our tone and speech toward the animals in our care keeps them stuck in an emotionally immature state, which can lead to anxiety. There is a reason that one in two dogs die of cancer and over 75 percent of them struggle with anxiety; it has a great deal to do with the emotional burden placed on them to regulate the very people who should be teaching them how to regulate themselves. How we speak to them plays a huge role in their ability to feel their feelings separate from ours and create inner stability for themselves.

Baby talk can be defined here as anything spoken in a higher-pitched tone that reduces the animal to someone "less than" able to understand us on our own perceived level. Truthfully, the animal can perceive you at a level far beyond most of our current understanding, which is ironic. Baby talk is not the only type of speech this principle addresses, however. Basically, anything at all that is used to control, manipulate, reduce, and so on must be transformed into words that hold more respect and reverence for those in our care. Speak to them the way you would want to be spoken to or the way you would speak to a trusted, respected other. You will be blown away at how much calmer and more willing to listen they become when the energy behind your words is reverent of who they actually are rather than our conditioned perceptions.

This principle also includes no longer talking "through" or about the animal for entertainment, especially when the animal is present. Often, when humans gather around animals, we like to give them voiceovers. It can be fun, for sure, but it's not very respectful or loving, and it certainly doesn't demonstrate a high degree of maturity or presence. More often than not, this type of behavior occurs when the humans involved are uncomfortable dropping into intimate and authentic conversation with one another.

We can't raise emotionally mature dependents if we ourselves are not demonstrating emotional maturity, but when our animals behave in emotionally immature ways, they are often met with frustration. The animals only reflect the emotional development of their primary caregivers. They are not able to live autonomous enough lives to do anything else. Paying attention to what they are saying about our inner state is far more valuable than anything they can make us feel.

The layers to each of these principles seem never ending, but there's one more that must be addressed here as a baseline. Another commonly overlooked form of exploitation in regards to animals is objectification around their appearance. We find value in what we deem beautiful or cute, but what does cuteness really mean when we're using it to refer to a captive dependent in our care? The value we place on others being "cute" has nothing to do with that individual's actual needs; rather, it reflects our own, so I invite you to deeply consider what it means to be "cute," and who that's really about. What is the cost of having your worth attached to someone's perception of your appearance, especially when you're in the vulnerable position of being dependent on them for your care?

So Below

The energy behind baby talk is a lot more harmful than most people realize, in that the underlying motivation behind it is driven by trauma. It is always manipulative or controlling in some way when applied to a dependent animal, which needs mature modeling to become emotionally mature. Baby talk arises from someone's resistance to being accountable and responsible for themselves. It is an unconscious desire to remain childlike or reclaim the innocence or unburdened experience of childhood. Interestingly enough, it is also nearly always a projection of our current emotional state, which is why it so often feels uncomfortable to be around.

When I teach this work in person, when we get to this principle, I often invite my students to spend 5–10 minutes using only baby talk with one another. It does not take long to realize why this behavior is so disastrous to those in our care, and for our own evolution as well. No one being spoken to like this is actually being seen. They are simply being projected upon, and the body lets us know very quickly how out of alignment this behavior feels. To be a captive dependent consistently spoken to in this manner is to rarely be seen at all, and no one thrives in the absence of being fully recognized for who and what they are.

The difference between baby talk and authentically loving sweet, intimate speech can be clearly felt in the body. One is anxious, the other is calm. Always check in with the body to know where you're coming from in your interactions.

Practical Examples

- Be mindful of your tone. Are you trying to elicit a specific reaction or offering unconditional love? Trying to control or trying to understand?

- Instead of saying how "cute" someone is, try speaking more directly to how you feel in their presence. It is rarely about them anyway.

- Acknowledge the animals in your care for their character and qualities, rather than their surface-level appearance. See how they respond differently.

- When you catch yourself speaking to your animals from an anxious place, try to pause and take a breath. Say it again, in a different way, from a calmer place. Notice what happens.

Always Create a Space of Invitation

As Above

One of the most frustrating things an animal can do is demand our attention by jumping on us, pawing us, barking at us, biting us, or even clawing us to get what they want. Ever wonder where they learned that? Most people reach for and touch the captive dependent animals in their care without any consideration of that individual's right to bodily autonomy. When animals are touched without permission, and for the benefit of their caregivers, they simply demonstrate the behavior they've been taught. Unfortunately, they usually get punished or reprimanded for it, which is an incredibly confusing experience for them, since they are only following the example that has been set.

This principle is the most important precedent that can be set for the total transformation of the relationship and for restoring an animal's connection to their own voice and sense of personal power. All domesticated animals are operating on some level of learned helplessness, or unconscious acceptance of powerlessness. And it's no wonder.

Imagine you're a puppy that has just been brought home to a new family. Within the first 24 hours of being in your new home, hands have been placed on you in all manner of ways and primarily for the enjoyment of those now responsible for your care and development. How long would it really take to lose your sense of self if everyone was allowed to touch you simply because it made them feel good to do so?

Touching captive dependent animals for our own benefit is probably one of the most deeply destructive things we can do in terms of how we affect their ability to self-regulate and be emotionally independent. Aggression and anxiety are largely born from not respecting an animal's bodily autonomy. The degree to which they trust our leadership, rather than our offerings, is also born from here.

The idea behind this principle is to always, always give the animal the opportunity to say No to anything that isn't absolutely necessary for their immediate care and well-being. Because our influence over them is enormous, it is incredibly easy to manipulate them into saying Yes to what we want, but that's why we have the other principles to check ourselves. First, do no harm. Control only what is yours to control. Expect nothing.

In the beginning, the "space of invitation" is a literal physical space, created to give the animal the opportunity to decide whether or not they wish to engage. It is always surprising to people how often an animal will say No to an advance when allowed the chance to do so. The more No's you get, the stronger the individual you will raise. When we value loving those in our care more than using them, every No becomes a victory of some sort. It either means the animal feels confident enough to use their voice, or they are reflecting something out of alignment with our request that we can notice and recalibrate our response to, when appropriate.

Remember: Every time an animal invades your personal space, they are demonstrating how they, themselves, have had their boundaries violated repeatedly. Be accountable and responsible for that, rather than making them responsible for behavior they were conditioned into. Animals have healthy and considerate boundaries when their primary caregivers demonstrate their own.

So Below

When interacting with animals in our care, our energy is either directed outward, toward them; stays within us; or draws them into us. The drawing-in is the invitation. It feels safe and inviting, without attachment or expectation. It feels, first and foremost, voluntary. I've heard a qi gong master describe this as "moving so that the air (animal, in this case) becomes fascinated with you."

This is where trust is built in the relationship. Invitation is vulnerable, allowing. It can be rejected, and it should be any time it feels like a No won't be respected. Your invitation is only true and trustworthy when there is no desperation behind it. This is what makes emotionally mature animals want to know and be close to you, including those in the wilderness. Fascination is often met with fascination, and that's where magic can happen.

Practical Examples

- Extend your hand, and pause, offering physical space, before making contact. Do not make contact unless the animal demonstrates an obvious Yes. As a new, healthier relationship builds and real intimacy is achieved, this space will get smaller and smaller, but for most people it needs to be significant in the beginning.

- Do not ask for contact from a captive, dependent animal. They are not responsible for you. Your offerings should be for their benefit, not yours.

- If we mindlessly take away an animal's mobility for our own convenience or benefit, they will no doubt become further disconnected from their own voice. The smaller the animal is, the more mindful we need to be in this work. Do not pick up and carry an animal just because you can or want to. Only do so in situations where you have earned their trust and they desire it, or when it's absolutely necessary for their safety and well-being.

Honor Every No

As Above

The individuals in our care should always feel free and safe enough to express themselves and tell us No, if something is not working for them. As a former trainer, this is the very opposite of how I was conditioned to relate to animals. My life was about looking for the Yes, and getting what I wanted from the animals in my care; conditioning them to be and behave exactly the way I wanted.

Love is about looking for the No and respecting it, no matter what. Most domesticated animals don't feel empowered enough to even attempt to say No, or when they do, it is because they've been pushed so far beyond their limits that it comes out as something extreme, like aggression. Any sort of aggressive behavior or extreme defensiveness happens well beyond the animal's first sign of No. For many domesticated animals, simply freezing in place is the most empowered No they can offer before being pushed to the point of protecting themselves. I cannot tell you how many times I have heard the words "Oh, if my animal didn't like it, they would definitely let me know" from someone defending their desire to exploit the animals in their care.

The truth is, most people have no idea what the subtlest forms of No even look like. A deeply conditioned animal will never offer an obvious No, and you can't honor a No you do not wish to look for. It was learning how to recognize all forms of No that made me realize I needed to change everything in relationship to the animals I loved.

In 2017, I taught Sanctuary13 to an audience for the first time at an international horse festival in New Zealand. This particular principle was one of my demonstrations. As I described the elements to the crowd, a buckskin gelding munched contentedly on the grass nearby. I told the audience I was about to approach the horse, and I wanted them to silently determine his first No. After attempting an interaction that I knew he would say No to because I purposely and subtly did not make my energy safe or inviting, I turned back to the audience and asked them to share with me at what point they noticed his No. Not a single person was able to recognize the first one, which was him ignoring my obvious intention to interact. It wasn't until he physically moved away from me that they saw a No. Many horse people believe that a No is something as extreme as biting, kicking, or bucking, which happens only after countless softer No's have been ignored.

Your best bet for recognizing a No from an animal is to assume that No is anything that isn't an obvious Yes. An obvious Yes always looks like a moving toward the invitation (which must be there!), even if it's subtle. Even a micro-movement toward you still counts as Yes, but a micro-movement away from you, or even a freeze, is always No. To honor the No means to at least acknowledge it through recognition, and to always respect it fully by disengaging from any activity that isn't absolutely necessary for the animal's immediate care and well-being. You only get to override a No when it comes to necessary care that must be carried out in the animal's best interest, which as the caregiver, you ultimately get to decide. However, as I often tell my students, an animal will never say No to something that is genuinely in their best interest. What they say No to is how you approach them about it.

So Below

Nonhuman animals do not have conceptual opinions about their No. They simply move away from what doesn't feel good and safe and move toward what does. We can learn a lot from that. Receiving a No from an animal is a gift of awareness that often offers an invitation to reflect more deeply around our own motivations and emotional alignment, but also allows us to move beyond conditioning into deeper wisdom around what we believe.

An empowered animal will usually say No to fearful energy in a caregiving situation. Many of my students have sought help with examples of animals being hard to bathe, hard to get their nails or hooves trimmed, or difficult to manage in veterinary situations or when high anxiety is present. Most of the No's in those situations involve the emotional state of the caregiver. No animal is going to trust you if you feel anxious about what you're asking of them. To gain cooperation in these situations, we must be clear and confident about what we are asking or are about to do to the animal. If you're clear and calm and you still get a No, it is a great opportunity to challenge conditioned beliefs around what our animals "need." I cannot tell you how much my animals have taught me to disregard entirely or do differently in regard to their care or how many vet bills I've avoided by actually listening to them.

Practical Examples

- When you reach for an animal, even if you forget the space of invitation, try to be mindful of whether or not they want your touch. Withdraw it entirely if they don't.

- Instead of demanding compliance when a request is ignored, pause to reflect if your request was even appropriate. If it is, make sure your energy is calm and confident and then ask again, but do not try to turn a No into a Yes.

- Always be willing to ask "Is this really necessary?" when an animal says No to something you're asking or trying to do.

Your Boundaries Are
Your Responsibility

As Above

In codependent or emotionally enmeshed relationships, it is the absence of healthy and appropriate boundaries that leads to inner turmoil and dysfunction. It took a lot of pain and suffering for me to finally experience and understand that boundaries were actually a much stronger demonstration of love than affection. Boundaries are absolutely necessary for the proper development of a true sense of self and connection to one's own soul and emotional guidance.

When our attention is too focused on another's experience, or too allowing of theirs into our own, we lose sight of our own path and purpose. When this happens between a guardian and a dependent, it often has devastating results for the dependent, and is one of the most destructive and insidious forms of unintended abuse.

In a training or domesticated mindset, we make others responsible for our needs and boundaries. One can get away with this behavior for a while in a functionally codependent relationship between equals, but it makes no sense in the power dynamic between a guardian and their dependent. Imagine the inner confusion caused to a captive dependent animal that is brought into someone else's life where they are dependent on that individual for their basic needs but are expected to behave in complete opposition to what is being demonstrated to them on a daily basis. For example, someone acquires a horse for the purpose of ignoring that animal's bodily autonomy to climb on top of them, but if that horse steps too close to them on the ground, the horse is reprimanded for not "respecting" the person's physical space. How sane and confident can someone really become in that setting? At best, they become an emotionally suppressed individual who is compliant but operating in a deep state of learned helplessness for the sake of some sense of peace in their lives in exchange for cooperation.

On the surface, this principle addresses the responsibility we have toward those we bring into our care to be responsible for our own physical safety rather than expecting them to do it for us, especially when they are in a conditioned state. Domesticated animals only violate boundaries when their own boundaries have been violated. We have to learn how to be accountable for this and understand the influence we have over them. Getting angry at an animal for jumping on us, stepping on us, or otherwise invading our space is not helpful; being present enough with them to move out of the way and be responsible for our energy is.

Your needs are your business, and not the responsibility of those in your care, or anyone else for that matter, once you are no longer a dependent yourself. We only mature when we become accountable and responsible for ourselves. Setting appropriate boundaries does not look like making someone else wrong for their behavior or judging/reacting to them for it. It does look like being clear about what does and doesn't work for you, maintaining composure, and being willing to take responsibility for the space you need. In many cases, that may practically look like walking away from a situation, but in a guardian/dependent dynamic, you don't get to abandon someone in your care. You simply create the space that is needed without making them responsible for it.

This is another place where neutral, physical boundaries can be very helpful until the maturity is there for the relationship to thrive. If you do not know how to communicate or set boundaries without control, something like a fence can be very useful for spending time with someone safely until you understand each other. A friend once described boundaries in the best way I've yet to hear, which was referring to them as "the space I need to stay present with you." Love is presence, and

boundaries make presence possible until we restore connection to it fully.

So Below

Physical boundaries are only necessary until we learn to master our energy. No one invades our space without the energetic invitation to do so. Even predators cannot engage with prey unless the energy is present, usually in the form of fear, to invite one into a conversation. That doesn't mean the prey is agreeing to be preyed upon; it simply means they engaged. Your attention is your strongest ally in creating strong boundaries. When your attention is deeply focused on yourself and your inner world, while maintaining awareness of your surroundings, you do not invite unwanted advances.

For example, it matters not whether you are sending someone positive or negative attention. Once you are focused on them, you've invited them into the conversation. The most demonstrable way of teaching this has been in relationship to dogs that are overexcited to greet someone or jumping on them. If one reacts with judgment, fear, or anger, their attention is on the dog rather than on themselves. All it takes, and I mean this seriously, is redirecting that attention fully and firmly back to self and into one's own body, and within just a few seconds, the animal will disengage and leave you alone. Your attention is incredibly powerful for manifesting your experience. Relating to animals in this way will set you up with the skills to live a life of deliberate creation if you choose to recognize your power.

We feed whatever we focus on. Boundaries cannot be properly set in judgment of another. They only get clearly communicated when we are focused on creating them from a sense of our own needs, rather than what we expect from someone else, and this is what most often results in them being respected. If you're not feeding an energetic connection to someone, they are pretty unlikely to stay interested in you.

Practical Examples

- If you walk into a friend's house, and their dog starts jumping on you or ramming their nose into delicate spaces, bring your focus fully into your own body. Your thoughts and attention cannot be on the dog, only your inner experience and where your body needs to move, if necessary. If you're thinking about or judging the dog, you're inviting them in, whether you want to or not.

- Your hands and body can act as a neutral, physical boundary in extreme circumstances, but only if your emotional experience remains neutral; otherwise, you're just going to be defending yourself from an advance you're inviting through your attention.

- You're sitting on the couch, and a cat casually jumps into your lap without invitation. Without reacting emotionally, calmly scoot out from under or gently lift the cat from your lap. Someone taught them to ignore your bodily autonomy by example, and if it's your cat, that someone was you. Be accountable for that, and begin to set a different, more loving example.

- If you're spending time with horses, be responsible for where you place your body, and present to when and if you need to move out of the way to avoid getting hurt.

Everyone Is Always Right

As Above

As a horse trainer, the most important belief I ever adopted was "The horse is always right." I first heard those words from Mark Rashid, and they later became paramount in applying my learning with Nevzorov Haute Ecole (NHE), though the concept was much more evolved in NHE. Before NHE, I used the understanding behind this affirmation to manipulate horses and others into giving me what I wanted. It was an incredibly useful tool for turning No into Yes, as long as you had more power in the relationship.

When I changed my approach, the intention behind the principle was different but the underlying meaning remained the same: Given everyone's unique perspective, background, and experiences, we all act in ways that are appropriate for us at all times. Arguing with that is a sure-fire recipe for conflict rather than connection, and completely disregards the valid reasons behind someone else's behavior.

Meeting someone where they are at, without any agenda to change them, is how we love them. It is also the only way a safe, unconditional container is created for real change to occur. When we are responsible for our own boundaries, we do not need to try to change anyone else, much less agree with them. The degree to which we want someone to behave differently from what they are reflects the degree to which we are refusing to be responsible for ourselves.

Dependent animals only know how to behave in ways that are biologically appropriate for their species and that reflect how they have been guided by their human caretakers and the trauma of domestication. They are dependents; their behavior has been mostly influenced by those with power over their lives, rather than a decision arising from their own sense of self. Making them wrong for anything serves no one, unless, that is, the goal is to exploit them.

No matter how the animals in our care behave, we must choose to meet them with understanding, compassion, and boundaried attention if we want them to mature and if we also want to eliminate obstacles to our own growth. When working with animals that have experienced serious trauma resulting in major behavioral challenges, this degree of accountability is especially necessary, in order to help them heal. We are all just trying to get by with the knowledge we have at the time, doing what we think we must in order to survive. With so much power over the lives of the animals in our care, we are responsible for creating the container within which healing can occur, for becoming a safe space for our animals to deal with whatever is going on inside.

We only make others "wrong" when we are disconnected from our own sense of authentic power. Attempting to control someone through judgment or our position in their lives is a coping mechanism for insecurity. How we behave on the surface matters little if what we're feeling while we're acting that way is incongruent. To avoid making the other person "wrong" involves more than not voicing our opinion; it's about owning our emotional response to them and taking responsibility for it. A primary caregiver need not do or say anything at all to make someone in their care feel reduced in some way. We know when someone is upset with us or directing emotion at us, even when it isn't named.

A fulfilling relationship and cooperation based on trust is not possible to achieve through power plays or shame. If you love someone, meet them where they're at, with deep understanding and compassion, and watch how they bloom without any desire from you to do so. Doing so requires complete responsibility for how one feels.

So Below

The underlying lesson from this principle is to understand the role of emotional triggers and what they actually mean in relationship to others. All triggers are trauma responses. We can only be triggered by emotions for which we have not yet developed mature processing skills. In this regard, a "trigger" is an intense emotional reaction. Once trauma is healed, and we feel able to fully feel and process specific emotions, they are far more subtle experiences, resulting in discernment rather than judgment.

The difference between discernment and judgment is our reaction. Discernment looks and feels like observing, making an assessment, and calmly deciding what action to take in response, if any. It is peaceful and comes from a place of authentic power. Judgment is more of a knee-jerk reaction, which leaves us feeling disempowered and blaming something outside ourselves for our experience. Judgment results from not getting our needs met, and those needs are not anyone else's responsibility, but most especially not the responsibility of a dependent in our care.

Every emotion we feel in relationship to someone else is born from our unique perspective and needs and is not attached to the individual to whom we are reacting. Emotion is our soul speaking to us, trying to guide us. It has little to do with another, beyond the moment we are in and how we feel in relationship to them, and even then, it is still more a reflection of ourselves than the other. The more emotionally mature we become, the less reactive we are to anything outside us. Instead, we become powerfully able to respond with integrity.

Practical Examples

- An animal snaps at you. Take a step back, feel whatever comes up in your body without turning it into judgment or reaction (maintain composure), and meet them with compassion and understanding. It wasn't about you; it was about their needs. As their caregiver, you are responsible for their needs. Seeing and hearing them is the first step to figuring out what need is being expressed.

- Do not yell at or verbally condemn the animals in your care. They do not understand being made "wrong" by their caregivers. An emotionally mature animal sets boundaries but doesn't make the other wrong through judgment.

- You can only meet someone as deeply as you've met yourself. If you are judging someone else's behavior, it's time to have a compassionate conversation with your own inner critic and look for ways to accept yourself where you're at, so you can show up in the same way for those in your care.

- Trust that your animals may actually know more than you do about a great many things. Give them the benefit of the doubt when they behave in ways you do not yet understand. They are far more connected to what it is we're working on remembering.

Be Willing to Meet Your Own Needs

As Above

No one who has been domesticated emerges into adulthood assuming responsibility for their own needs. Unfortunately, making that painful shift is the only way we step into wholeness and emotional maturity, realigning with soul. It isn't fair to have to do that on our own, which deserves to be felt and acknowledged. In our earliest development, we were designed to be guided through the process by caring, emotionally mature caregivers, but that didn't happen, so here we are. If we can get support from those with equal power and the ability to consent, it sure makes things easier, but at the very least, we must be willing to show up and care for ourselves.

Most humans spend their entire lives seeking out some level of codependency with others or relying on controlling external circumstances in order to function. What most people refer to as "needs" are actually "desires" in order to avoid feeling the pain of trauma. Actual needs are pretty basic but include the one thing most of us have been deprived of: learning how to feel the full extent of our feelings.

Pets are kept to fulfill an emotional support role, regardless of whether or not they've been trained or certified to do so. A dependent depends on their primary caregiver to model emotional regulation, not use them for it. They cannot bear the weight of such a burden in any sort of sustainable way. Our use of captive dependent animals for emotional regulation has to stop if inner healing is to take place. Self-soothing through animals only addresses the symptoms while creating long-lasting consequences for everyone involved.

Instead of reaching for dependent animals, we have to learn how to attune ourselves to see what is actually needed. Ultimately, beyond biological needs, we just need to feel our feelings, but that's a lot harder than it sounds if we haven't learned how to stay in the body long enough to commit to whatever process arises. Even if we frame surface-level desires as "needs," we have to be willing to inquire what those needs are. We can begin by asking, "What would support me in this moment?" and "How can I offer that to myself?" Sometimes it is as simple as coaching ourselves through a thought process. Other times, it might be physically embracing ourselves using safe, intimate touch to self-soothe.

Accepting and asking for help from an appropriate source is not only healthy but sometimes a necessary step if we are to acquire the skills needed to facilitate difficult processes. The key is to make sure we are not reaching for help from a place of avoidance. At the end of the day, we all have to learn how to feel our own feelings, and no one can actually help with that; they can only provide supportive space and offer helpful tools to make the experience less difficult. Any technique or tool used to self-regulate can either take us more deeply into experiencing our emotions fully to support growth or used to bypass feelings until the next time they arise. Each of us has to choose between treating symptoms of trauma or actually healing it.

So Below

The energetic component of meeting our own needs is simply being fully present to whatever emotional experience is taking place within us and understanding that is our greatest need. The need to feel better or feel differently than what we're feeling is an idea that keeps us vulnerable to outside control and manipulation.

When we have a healthy relationship with the full range of emotional experience, we are not good consumers and cannot be influenced easily by someone else's agenda. Recognizing and embracing the fullness of our feeling capacity is how we step into complete authentic power and regain authority over our ability to respond, rather than react to what the world presents to us. Being able to feel it all obviates any need for domestication because it elevates our awareness and creates evolved solutions for our own kind and all life on the planet.

Practical Examples

- Hug yourself—really hug yourself the way you need to be held. It's awkward at first, but sometimes it's exactly what we need. Do it with love, say the things you need to hear and touch your own body with the kindness you deserve. It's mind-blowing how effective something so simple can be.

- Write it out. Get your feelings on paper, and allow tears to flow if they will.

- Go for a walk, dance, or stretch. Move in whatever way your body desires, while being mindful of what is asking to be acknowledged inside.

- Make yourself a beautiful, nutritious meal. Don't hold back, take time to prep, cook, and sit down without distraction to enjoy and honor your body. This single act of nurturance can change everything about how much we feel supported in life.

- Invest in healing bodywork from a skilled facilitator. Sometimes being in a full state of surrendered receptivity can unlock major emotional blocks that are harder to access alone.

Remember to Play

As Above

Healthy, happy animals have something in common—they play! Play is a vital part of maintaining balance in our lives, and it's also a key component to accessing deeper levels of connection with those we love. When play isn't present in our lives, it's a major indicator that we are dissatisfied with our lives and low in vitality. Loving relationships only thrive when there is time spent together simply for fun and enjoyment, getting us into the shared experience of having a body and remembering that life doesn't have to be so serious all the time. The experience of playing together forms deep connections with the parts of ourselves that have not been conditioned by time and experience.

Authentic play is not rigidly structured or about winning or achieving some goal; it's about the experience of relating from a place of open exploration, curiosity, and awe. Play can include rules or agreements, but it is left open to organic expansion as long as it feels voluntary and life-affirming to everyone involved, thereby adding supportive energy to those engaged. When playing with a dependent animal, it is important to remember the power dynamic and our responsibility toward them and, therefore, let them lead the way. Let them show you what they think is interesting, and allow yourself to be amazed by their willingness to share it with you and where that may lead. Play requires vulnerability, which removes limits on what can be discovered through the experience, as long as the container is kept safe so that everyone can feel and express authentically.

With domesticated animals that are still carrying a lot of trauma, we must become aware of the difference between play and imbalanced behavior used to cope with stress. Play comes from a place of joy and well-being, not anxiety. A dog with obsessive fixations, for example, is not trying to play. He is trying to escape his inner discomfort through distraction, essentially demonstrating an addiction that can only be addressed through authentic connection. Engaging in obsessive behaviors with such an animal distances healing; bring presence to them, instead, and slowly build into authentic play as they are able to go there. Authentic play always, always feels like an invitation. It must be voluntary.

Play involves deep listening, especially when playing with an animal that doesn't speak the same language as you. Eventually, you will join them in a language older than words, once you remember it. The more you can stay open and really listen to what they want you to understand, the more fun you can have together. Just make sure to keep all coercion, manipulation, and control out of it. Restorative play does not require instigation; only a safe invitation to follow wherever the conversation leads among its participants.

So Below

Play feels like open discovery in the body; the awe of open-ended investigation and curiosity. It does not arise from knowing or ambition; only the desire to explore and experience and connect. Play is the practice of finding the courage to embrace the unknown with enthusiasm and interest in what might happen next. Remember these qualities before you engage, so as not to turn the experience into something less than restorative.

Practical Examples

- Take things slowly. Play is an exploration, not just a means to release pent-up energy.

- If an animal seems too shut down to engage, create an invitation to play by being safe but silly. For instance, sometimes I will do something an animal has not seen me do before to spark their curiosity, like rolling around slowly on the ground.

- Make sure your energy is drawing them in, instead of being directed outward. Play with a dependent animal should feel like an invitation being extended to them, and vice versa.

Drop the Story

As Above

To inhabit the body more fully, less attention must be given to the mind. This principle originated from witnessing and experiencing Denali become new, expanded versions of herself repeatedly within the container I was offering of unconditional love and acceptance. She would not have been able to rise to her potential if I had been maintaining a story of limitation about who she was or could become. That is equally true of the stories we choose to keep believing about ourselves.

"Dropping the story" is about releasing our attachment to believing our thoughts and being willing to stay open. Let experience rather than opinion guide you. We attach firmly to thoughts for a sense of control, but it always limits perception. Our stories hold us back when they aren't used consciously for learning and enjoyment.

The stories that cause us to get stuck are often unconscious and disempowering, the result of making assumptions or not challenging old patterns of thought or belief. While it may be interesting and even helpful in some circumstances to know the details of one's past, there is a fine line between facts and letting those facts own you in the here and now. We are not our trauma or what happened to us, and neither are the animals in our care. As long as we are attached to our own stories or stories about those we love, we are held captive by them.

I once met the sweetest young dog whose guardian assured me that she was "afraid of towels." Because of this, they avoided showing her towels or triggering the resulting anxiety that would ensue. Fortunately, I had some time to be alone with this young, traumatized pup, and came to understand that the towel was just the trigger and the trauma had nothing to do with the towel itself.

I created a solid and safe container of nonreaction that allowed her to interact with the towel. Her trigger came, she was overwhelmed with fear, but because I was fully present and not afraid of her experience, I was able to stay with her until it passed. As a result, she got to have the experience of that emotion moving fully through her body, and on the other side, she was no longer afraid of the towel. Her experience with the towel had been rewired, but that was only possible because of how safe the space had been for her to experience the intense emotions without risk of retraumatization.

That space can only be held by someone who isn't reacting to the trigger or feeling fearful themselves. What more commonly happens in those scenarios is that someone sees another being suffering, buys into that suffering, takes it on themselves, and strengthens the story of whatever they perceive is causing the suffering. Suffering only happens as a result of not being willing to feel difficult feelings without resistance, usually resulting from believing a story that says "I shouldn't be experiencing this" or "This is bad." When we can accept reality in the moment we're in, without needing it to be different, that's when we become empowered to change it, but from inspiration rather than fear.

We don't need to do a lot of thinking, especially when we aren't consciously choosing to use our minds in a deliberate way. We need to be more like other animals, fully inhabiting our bodies, where internal wisdom can arise. Instead, most humans are leading lives guided by the conditioned thoughts that were programmed through their own domestication. Thinking can be addictive, keeping us in swirling patterns of familiar emotion as a means to avoid the feelings we are more afraid of. Unresolved trauma that creates stuck patterns of emotion in the body often results in repetitive thought patterns. It's remarkable to learn that if we'll just feel those feelings, the thoughts disappear because the underlying energy producing them has been released.

Story can be valuable when used on purpose for enjoyment or education. Beyond that, story is mostly a distraction to avoid feeling what's present and dealing with it effectively.

When I work with students directly, I'm always amazed by the wide range of story available to keep someone out of an emotional experience. When we were dependents, that coping mechanism was a survival tactic that probably served and protected us during a time when we did not have control over our own lives. As self-aware adults, we must be willing to challenge and release attachment to those old stories if we want to move through and heal the trauma. We surely cannot expect to help the animals in our care heal when we have not done the work to heal ourselves.

So Below

Dropping the story is not about stopping all the thoughts in our heads; it is about dropping our attention off the mind and back into the body, releasing the energetic attachment to those thoughts. What's the hidden motivation behind the story that's been shared? Why is that story important to you? What is the value in sharing that story about someone in your care, and how might it be limiting their experience in some way? Question, question, question. That is how we begin to dismantle the attachment and drop the stories running our lives and the lives of those in our care. Healing is two-fold. It is both being able to feel the full spectrum of emotion and also deliberately challenging and reprogramming our conditioned thoughts and behavioral patterns through consistent practice.

Practical Examples

- Try to stop using the word "rescue" to describe someone you love. That's about you not them. It is much more supportive of those we love to share the qualities of their character than to keep them limited to what's happened to them or what we've done for them.

- Animals don't live in story. When they display emotional discomfort in our care, we create more discomfort for them when we attach story to their experience and keep them stuck in it because of our influence over their lives.

- Pay attention to what you say about the animals in your care. Your perception of them plays a huge role in their experience. When you decide who someone is, based on what you believe to be true about them, you limit who they can become.

Feel It All

As Above

Were it not for the deeply conditioned thoughts and behavioral patterns surrounding our individual and collective trauma, it would be simple to just say "Feel it all" is the only principle you really need to know. It is true, though. All of this work and all of these words are only leading you to this one principle: Feel it all. The previous principles are about clearing the space to do just that.

The most difficult, and important, part of this work is surrendering to emotion. We were never taught how. The nature of domestication does not support that process, because no one who can fully experience emotion can be easily used or controlled. We are terrified not only of the experience itself but of whom we might become, what might have to change on the other side of it. Everything is waiting for you there, that's far scarier than living a predictable, unsatisfying life. Sometimes all it takes to find the courage we need to feel is to fully embrace how much we actually want to love the animals we brought into our lives. The interesting thing about feeling our feelings is that no matter what they are or how messy it gets, we actually feel better to be around in our authentic, emotionally congruent experience than when we're trying to protect ourselves from what is actually going on inside us.

The animals want to be with us for our realness more than they want to be with our fear. It's exploitative and destructive to use the animals in our care to bypass that fear. Experiencing it fully, within our own container, in their presence, however, is the most loving thing we have to offer them. To love someone is to show up fully present with them. To love a dependent is to model that degree of presence. When we are present, we are going to feel the feels. All the principles before this one are simply guidelines for creating a container for presence to arise.

We cannot feel it all when we are engaged in any of the behavior that the first 12 principles work to eliminate. Those behaviors are distractions born from fear and attempts to control that which was never ours to control. When distraction is no longer available, all the emotions you've been running from will emerge, and you are presented with the opportunity to fully engage with them and step into the most authentically powerful version of yourself. That is who your dependents need you to be; that is who you deserve to become.

We can only lead effectively when we're not afraid to feel. Animals know this. They do not trust anyone or anything that is not deeply connected to their feeling body, and they shouldn't. Someone is trustworthy when they are in conversation with their soul, and emotion is the language of that conversation. "Feel it all" means feel *all* emotions. Courage is required here. You will survive your feelings—at least, the most real part of you will.

So Below

This principle lives below the surface of our external lives. Drop your awareness away from surface reality, including your thoughts, and into the rich experience of bodily sensation. We process and experience emotion by staying fully in the body. We stay fully in the body by keeping, or consistently returning, our attention to it. Do not assign meaning to the experience. Drop the story. Just stay with the feelings. Stay curious and open. If you need to know, insight will land, but not through seeking it.

It isn't our feelings we're so afraid of; it's the unknown territory they invite us to enter. Utilize whatever tools and techniques you are drawn to, as long as they help you go deeper into the experience of your emotions rather than bypassing them. It is more than okay to comfort yourself through the process; just don't pull yourself out of the process.

Practical Examples

- You reach out to touch your dog without remembering to create a space of invitation, but you catch yourself at the last moment and pause. You notice that you were reaching because you feel lonely and want connection. Withdraw your hand, and feel that loneliness. Drop your attention away from any thoughts surrounding it, and be fully with the sensations in the body.

- You've removed all forms of control from your relationship with your horse, and she wants nothing to do with you now. It makes you terribly sad. Feel that sadness. Drop your awareness away from the thoughts around it and into the sensations of the body. She'll probably be standing next to you when you're done crying.

- Allow yourself to grieve. Everything is changing, and there's a lot to feel in relationship to that. Drop your awareness away from your thoughts, and just be with what's there by keeping your attention on the sensations. Do not assign meaning. If you have tasks that need to be done, do them, but keep some awareness in your body, and don't feed distraction.

- You're now seeing all the obvious insanity surrounding you because you read this book and now you're pissed at its author. Drop your awareness away from the thoughts and into the sensations in your body. Feel it. Don't project it.

Recap

The complexity and nuance of each of these principles seems never-ending. I have tried to share them here concisely and in their most basic forms. That is more than enough to guide you from here on, as long as you commit to putting them into practice and allow that experience to take you the rest of the way forward. All it takes is ten minutes a day to change your whole life. Do your best to apply them throughout your day, but give yourself at least ten minutes of devoted practice, applying them all together in a concentrated way, every day. I can be found online for additional support and offerings if you need help, but trust yourself and your process.

The principles only work when applied simultaneously. Don't pick and choose. If something isn't working, see which principle is missing. Use them as a system to check in with any time you're stuck in any sort of relational situation. You usually won't have to get past the first few before finding something to clean up. As long as your immediate practical responsibilities are met for the safety and well-being of those in your care, you really just have to feel it all. The rest will take care of itself. On the next page, you'll find a list of the principles for quick reference. Your soul already knows how to interpret them.

⊙≫⊗≪⊙

Sanctuary13

First, Do No Harm

Control Only What Is Yours to Control

Expect Nothing

Love Is Not a Transaction

Speak Only with Reverence

Always Create a Space of Invitation

Honor Every No

Your Boundaries Are Your Responsibility

Everyone Is Always Right

Be Willing to Meet Your Own Needs

Remember to Play

Drop the Story

Feel it All

Chapter 15

INCURSION

It had been over 18 months since I had felt the stress and worry of a missing Denali. Now, she was gone in a way I had never faced before, and it was a lot more frightening, knowing she hadn't been carried away on her own four feet. I didn't waste much time looking for her in the vicinity, as instinct told me she wasn't there. Instead, I immediately picked up the phone and called our nearest neighbor, a horse rescue I had not become acquainted with since our move. My breath caught in my throat as I heard the words, "Let me check with one of our workers and call you back. I think I heard someone talking over the radio about a white dog being picked up a little while ago." My worst fear was confirmed when the phone rang a moment later. Denali had been taken less than an hour ago by a man in a blue truck. The search was on.

Anguish was my main feeling after 48 hours of constant searching without more answers. Somehow, there was still peace in the moments between the emotions and taking the next indicated step, but the pain was present. Watching my own mind through the process was interesting. When the sun or a gentle breeze hit my skin or I noticed the birds singing or even when I slowed down long enough to witness the incredible scenery around me, there was peace through immense sadness and concern.

I often wanted to feel guilty in those moments, but only right before I remembered that in faith and gratitude, true magic can happen. In my frightened despair, I still had one thing to hold on to, and that was everything she had taught me out in the forest about presence and feeling. The work that had changed Denali's and my relationship was ready to be put under real pressure, a lot more than a leash walk in the city, for sure.

Could practicing unconditional love make the situation hurt less or bring her home?

Leads were easy to come by. Since she was witnessed being taken, I knew a few things to look for, and with the help of the neighbors and one of my friends, the truck had been tracked down easily within the first 24 hours. Unfortunately, the guy driving the truck denied everything. After two different people stopped him on the road and questioned him, I wasn't convinced. Next, I was pulled over, speaking to a dear friend on the phone who does distance communication with animals, when I saw the truck in question drive by. I hung up the phone and hit the gas, following him into the area I was most afraid he would go.

There are remote subdivisions all around the area in which I lived that were all bought up over the past few years by a large group of people for the purpose of growing marijuana illegally. The situation had created a lot of controversy and fear in our community. I didn't know anything about the people involved, and I wasn't all that interested in what they were doing until one of them decided to take my dog. A latent prejudice wanted to emerge and protect me from my fear and anger, but somehow, I knew that if I let any of my Southern redneck conditioning filter into my current belief system, I might lose Denali forever.

As I pulled up to the gate where the blue truck was parked in the distance beyond, I paid close attention to the bigotry that tried to enter my consciousness, and I kindly reminded myself that it doesn't live in this heart.

I waited outside the man's gate for what seemed like hours. During that time, every other vehicle that passed revealed a person or persons watching me with heavy suspicion and cell phones immediately rising to inform others of my presence there. One woman even filmed me. When my suspect finally came out, I let him know who I was and what I was looking for. He was polite but noticeably nervous and obviously lying. I always want to see the best in people, and it's one of my downfalls at times, but for Denali's sake, I chose to believe in that moment that he had nothing to do with her disappearance. I needed to for there to be any chance of getting her back.

Before we had finished talking, a black truck pulled up aggressively, purposely blocking me in the dirt driveway. A very stern-looking man hopped out, barely making eye contact with me, before speaking in urgent, foreign hushed tones to the young man I had been questioning. He then turned to me and took one of my missing dog flyers before returning to his truck, where a big, black German shepherd was tied up in the back, and left.

It was clear he had been called because we were there, and in my gut, I believe he was making sure the younger and more nervous fella wasn't saying anything he shouldn't. It didn't matter. All that could legally be done at that point had been, and I had to let it go for the time being and trust that law enforcement would continue to investigate the situation while I pursued other options.

New leads kept me constantly on the move. I had several intuitive people on board to help, including my trusted interspecies communication friend, as well as two other psychic professionals whose services were paid for by friends in the periphery. I had been to all the obvious places and made all the necessary calls to surrounding shelters, law enforcement agencies, and media outlets, and I had used my social media platform to let the whole world know to be on the lookout for the wild, fuzzy person I was responsible for. The pressure was really on if the guy in the blue truck had taken her, but in the meantime, I was consumed with following every other clue.

In the few, sacred moments of downtime, I surrendered entirely to my feelings as I had learned to do on the trail, quietly sobbing out my sadness without losing hope. Then I'd shake it off the way Denali taught me and get back to picking up the scent, following intuition or whatever guidance might show up. The signs were everywhere. They ranged from a white GMC Denali truck with a Husky brand generator sitting in the bed, to a kind man from Montana with a husky by his side who kept a lookout for hours under a bridge where I fully believed she might emerge if she followed the river someone said they saw her by.

I had what seemed like a limitless supply of energy and faith, and the only thing I can attribute it to is, in every moment, I was going over the principles of the work I had been applying in my relationship to Denali. It was the first time I realized that unconditional love was meant to be applied in relationship to EVERYTHING, not just other beings. I was using the principles of my work in relationship to the situation, to the people involved (including the person who took her), and most definitely to myself. I have no doubt that that is where my strength and resilience came from during those days.

The most challenging part of the process was that I knew that what was happening on the surface wasn't the most important thing I needed to pay attention to. Many people had stepped forward to help, but they were not aware of the energetic conversations going on below the guise of tangible leads and sightings. The guidance from my communicator friend, received directly from Denali, hit me in the gut as only a direct punch from truth can: that this was a lesson much bigger than what it appeared to be, about far more than someone taking a dog. It was a delicate balance of surrender, strength, and love that would determine what happened, not how fast I drove or who I questioned. This was my faith in the power of love put to the test, an invitation for me to step into the full integrity of what I believed.

As often as I fail in this area, this was not one of those times. My love for Denali was true and pure, and I was determined to put in my best effort, if it meant protecting her from a life less than the one of freedom promised her at home. I knew she could handle whatever came her way, even death, but I was willing to do whatever was necessary to get her back, including embracing the deepest level of trust I have ever known.

I had to accept that the only thing I needed to know or be in that moment was the love the animals had helped me come to understand. The details would sort themselves out. It was letting go of control to a degree I had yet to previously achieve, but I was allowing it to happen because I had those visceral memories of myself and Denali in that forest and how the connection between us only strengthened when I dropped all desire to force a result.

After days of driving checking up on every possible sighting or clue, I began to realize I couldn't keep putting every other aspect of my life on hold for the search. Every waking moment was spent looking for Denali or processing the emotions that needed to be released in order to keep going. By day five, every concrete detail had been followed up and exhausted or left pending a response. I turned more fully to the intuitive guidance of friends and professionals who had either been hired or had voluntarily reached out to help. Unfortunately, the most gifted ones all kept leading me back to the same conclusion; the one my gut had known all along.

Denali was close, and she was being held captive and in secret by those in relationship to the man who picked her up outside my fence. There was no way they didn't know where she belonged, as we had plastered the entire area with reward posters and been hypervigilant about letting it be known we were looking for her. I could not understand why anyone would not just return her, especially after the horse rescue offered an additional $1,100 reward on top of my own to help us get her back. What could someone possibly want with an older, spayed female dog that was an absolute nightmare to keep track of if you weren't willing to respect her?

At the height of my confusion about her dognapping, I started learning about the culture of the people I believed had Denali. It was clearly an organized effort to keep her hidden from me, and that was the most frustrating and difficult aspect to understand of all. Then I learned how America had used the older generations of this population in foreign wars. After their homeland was destroyed in the process, they were offered asylum in the United States, only to be treated like second-class citizens and have their trauma ignored. The prejudice and fear that was imposed on them daily from a community that had often made it clear they weren't welcome might have been more than enough to create a little hesitation to return my dog.

I began devoting some of my search time to understanding them more, including defending them from some of the incredible ignorance that was being posted on social media in response to Denali's disappearance. The comments I found the most disturbing were the accusations of her becoming someone's dinner, made in complete disgust by people who were very likely piling their own plates with the carcasses of different animals every night, oblivious to the irony.

People from all over stepped forward to help find Denali out of their "love" for animals while dishing out hate toward anyone who might be responsible for our loss. It was a complicated dance between being grateful for the help and not wanting to align with the motivation behind it, while doing my best to be an example of the alternative. Many people put energy into the effort to get her home, and I was grateful for the response, but it was the energy that Denali had taught me that was keeping the pathway open for something positive to emerge.

I knew where she was, but not specifically enough to access her safely or legally. By this time, the law had stopped caring about my missing dog and returned to their efforts to wage war on the plant that most of this group's dogs were used to protect. On day seven of the search, the 13th day of the month, I took my final call with a renowned animal psychic in Arizona. He proceeded to tell me all the things I already knew to be true but didn't want to hear. After a week of constantly devoted attention to getting her back, I knew it was time to let go and just trust.

I would never give up, but I had to start living my life again and being available to the other 26 animals in my care. Tears slowly rolled out the corners of both my eyes as I huffed in gentle sobs, listening to what this man had to say, and knowing surrender, trust, faith, and love were the only things left that could bring Denali home. I could not believe this was how it could end after finally learning how to love her in the way she deserved, but I had to trust that something bigger was at play, and despite it all, it would be for our highest good. I felt my whole body surrender to what was, and just as this conversation was about to end, I heard the tone of an incoming call.

Chapter 16
RESTORING THE CONNECTION

We are naturally and irrevocably connected to soul, but trauma causes distortion in the line of that connection. When we are unfamiliar with that deep, inner connection, we seek the experience of it outside ourselves, leaving us vulnerable to becoming dependent on outside sources and circumstances for any sort of stability in our lives. Even when we find stability that way, it is nearly impossible to stay in our authentic power through privilege alone. Trauma includes any gap in emotional development, and we all have it as a result of our own domestication. Trauma is not what happens to us, but rather, any area of emotional development left incomplete by our early conditioning.

Emotion is the language our soul uses to communicate with us about how we are perceiving whatever it is we are in relationship to at any given moment, including our thoughts. The body is the conduit for that communication. Keeping that channel of communication clear is how we receive the most valuable guidance for our lives, including the wild wisdom of instinct, intuition, and inspiration. It is also how we feel safe, connected, and at home within ourselves, no matter what is occurring outside us.

When we are not able to fully process and move emotion through our bodies, we feel the pain of severance. To fully restore the connection, we simply remove the obstacles keeping us from experiencing the full spectrum of emotion, and we stay with the process no matter how uncomfortable it may be until we emotionally mature. We don't reach emotional maturity until we find that staying power.

Ultimately, all of the principles of Sanctuary13 are leading us to the only thing we really need to master, which is how to feel all our emotions, so there is no longer a reason to avoid any of them or be controlled by outside forces. In order to do so, we must learn to stay in the body for the experience, and when we're first learning to deal with certain emotions that have been interrupted by trauma, the experience can be quite intense and painful, making us afraid to go there. Physical movement, when engaged with intimately and purposefully, is the key to learning how to stay present in and with the body while we adapt to allowing energy to move through.

The body is the gateway to restored and sustainable connection, but it's not as simple as maintaining outward appearances and health, or "blowing off steam" through physical activity. It is the inner body we must become intimately familiar with, and exercise alone is too external to get us there.

Practicing Sanctuary13 with other animals is only one piece of the puzzle toward ultimate healing, albeit a very important piece. Conscious movement practices, or the practice of Sanctuary13 in relationship to your own animal body, are the key to maintaining a soul conversation that keeps us from getting stuck in trapped emotion.

The domesticated mind takes a while to deprogram out of the conditioned thoughts that create unnecessary swirling vortexes of emotion. Deliberate and conscious, soul-aligned movement can take us deeply into the feelings to the point of resolving repetitive thought patterns altogether. Most repetitive thoughts that cause suffering are rooted in unresolved emotion anyway, so dealing with them at the source is the only way to be truly free of them. Otherwise, we can find ourselves swirling in emotion that is only being experienced because our thoughts are going uncontrolled, and that is very much not the point of Feel it All.

I never knew how to be and stay in my body before spending time with horses in the reverent way that led to Sanctuary13. In the physical presence of a horse, it had become easy for me to feel and process whatever came up, but outside of that container, it wasn't as accessible. I definitely didn't have a handle on it in the face of being triggered in relationship to other humans. There was so much healing left to be done, and I simply couldn't rely on being near animals to feel safe anymore. Once I was no longer using domestication as a distraction from myself, I was able to listen better to my soul's guidance on my next steps. The first place I landed was in a talk on sacred sexuality, where I hoped to learn how to address some of my deepest wounds.

The talk was given in Ashland, Oregon, by an incredible facilitator called Sarah Byrden. This was my initiation into a long journey of getting to know my own body as a safe space to call home. The sexuality work I did under her guidance changed my life in a huge way, but when it was combined with her wilderness work and a lineage of archetypal qi gong, an entirely new world of inhabiting my animal self became available. I was able to access, and then feel, deeply repressed emotions that simply wouldn't get triggered in my normal day-to-day life. The real catalyst for my growth in this area, however, came from meeting someone on a similar path with somatic practices: a brilliant woman named Jaye Marolla.

I met Jaye on my first wilderness immersion with Sarah. I was drawn to her immediately because she moved in the exact way I longed to live the entirety of my life—with precise and deliberate intention. The power of her presence was palpable, and I recognized a kinship there. It was easy to recognize our mutual commitment to personal evolution and soul. We became fast friends, and I still consider her one of the most important and influential people in my life.

Movement practice was the foundation of our time spent together, and I could not have been more grateful to have found someone I so trusted and respected to guide me into that world for the first time. From qi gong, Jaye introduced me to the highest quality lineages of yoga, martial movement, and even contact improvisation dance, which I would have been terrified of at any other point in my life.

Finding a home within my own body was the missing link to maintaining an open dialogue to emotion. In order to stay with emotion, we have to feel safe inside ourselves. Movement that takes us into the deepest kind of intimacy with ourselves is necessary if we are to engage with the fullness of this work. None of this is about doing the "right" thing with animals; it's about becoming the animals we were always designed to be, and removing the obstacles that keep us from restoring that connection.

After five months of friendship and practice with Jaye, I went to Vermont in my first attempt to fully restore my connection with the woman who had inspired me to change my life and relationship to animals back in 2012. The trip did not go how I wanted it to go, but that didn't matter because of who I had become.

Instead of being burdened by disappointment and attachment, I took myself up an icy, snow-covered mountain that January, during single-digit temperatures. In only my normal hiking boots, the trek up was challenging but not altogether difficult. The trip down, though, was revolutionary. I ran and slid most of the way down the mountain that day because, for the first time in my entire life, my body was strong enough, my core dependable enough, and my vitality intact enough to do so. It was one of the most joyful, liberating, and powerful experiences of my life. My body was so trustworthy and alive that I wondered how I could have ever wanted or needed the body of a horse to experience that kind of exhilaration in the past. When I got back to my vehicle, the first thing I did was call Jaye to express my gratitude and tears of joy for what she had helped me accomplish inside myself.

⊙»»⊙«‹‹⊙

PART THREE

>>>⊙<<<

HAVE COURAGE

Chapter 17

INTEGRATION

The incoming call went to voicemail as I took in the animal psychic's last message. "She is close and being held, but she wants to go home and is looking for the opportunity to run," he said. "She doesn't know how long it will take, but she won't give up, just like she knows you won't. You have a very strong connection with this girl." It was like slow motion, feeling my entire body release every ounce of tension it had been holding, allowing complete surrender as I ended the call.

I knew the feeling by now. It was the same as the moment with Shai when he changed my life forever, and it was the same as in the creek when Denali stopped running and returned to my side. Then, like every time before, a similar miracle unfolded in response. I listened to the voicemail. Denali was in a car, on her way home.

When the car pulled up, it was too good to be true. I was so out of balance and excited and emotional the moment she leapt from the open door, that she, in perfect Denali style, went to the man that returned her instead, because he was calm. Even in that moment, I appreciated her sincere devotion to truth, though, and especially, because I so desperately wanted to hug her and tell her how happy I was to see her again.

I noticed, laughed, and she ran over to me with the kind of composure I admire in her every single day, and then she smothered me in kisses. The man who returned her was not interested in the affection she offered him. He was too busy filming the entire event, most especially recording himself stating she had been taken by mistake, that his people were not interested in the reward, and that the man in the blue truck had nothing to do with any of it. He said it was a red truck that had taken her, out of concern for her safety, not blue. I was too happy to have my girl home to care, but I definitely felt the lie that time.

Composure was a lesson taught me by a stallion whose bite stung far less than the initial few times of learning not to react to it. Love can take the hit, and that's how deep truth gets communicated in return. Shai taught me that, Denali reinforced it, and that day I embodied it as I shared deep appreciation for her return even while anger made its presence known only to me in every cell of my body. I drank it in and let it strengthen my resolve to better protect those I love so dearly. Then I let it go and shook his hand. Compassion for the wounds of his people helped, but nothing would make me forget what we had been through that week.

Denali was suffering from a cough, a urinary tract infection, and had at least six small bullet holes in her when she was returned. Apparently, she resorted to murdering chickens to make her presence all the more unpleasant for her captors, but that was a small piece of the puzzle that reunited us. It took months to wrap my head around everything that had unfolded, and so many details are unlikely to ever be disclosed, but certain things were revealed to confirm how and why she made it home.

Two factors had the biggest impact on the results, at least on the surface. One was I had lived in one of those remote subdivisions when I first moved to California and had served on the board of directors for the property owners association. I reached out to my former board president for contacts that might be able to help me locate Denali in those neighborhoods. Ultimately, the serving president of the board ended up being the person who convinced someone to come forward with Denali. She accompanied the man who returned her that afternoon.

The second factor was revealed to be the way I had handled the matter publicly. Denali only got returned because I had made it so clear that I meant no harm toward those who took her. They spent a week deciding whether they believed me, but my commitment to love paid off. It wasn't a perfect alignment with love, no doubt, but a commitment of balance between striving for it and surrendering to its constant stream below conditioned perceptions of reality. I have no doubt that if I had behaved in the way my past conditioning had compelled me to, I would have never seen her again.

No part of me believes that Denali was taken with mal intent. I think a young, ignorant man saw a beautiful dog on the road and took her without any concern for where she belonged or who might be missing her. When it became apparent that she had a family out looking for her, it was fear that kept him from returning her, complicated by incredibly deep layers of cultural, political, and legal concerns.

The day after her return, my phone rang. It was the man in the blue truck, and he sounded nervous again. I had not spoken to him since that initial confrontation the day after Denali's disappearance, but he had suddenly developed a keen concern for her well-being, calling to ask if I had ever found her and telling me he had been worried about her. I knew why he was calling, and I knew who had directed him to do so, but I played the game and relieved his feigned concern with my sincere gratitude to have her home. My internal lie detector grew enormously in the week she was gone, which meant her lessons were really sinking in.

After a trip to the vet and lots of gentle care from her family, Denali was back to herself, our bond even stronger than before. Her presence in my life is a constant reminder that love—authentic, unconditional, present love—is the greatest power we have access to if we learn how to surrender and work with it.

Denali embodies that powerful energy as much or more than anyone I've ever known, most especially as someone who lives within captivity. Because of that, she reminds me that the only limitation is in perception, so long as the essence of who we are is not compromised or shrouded by domestication. To love someone unconditionally is to set them free, even within the confines of their life circumstances. There are no walls, fences, or borders that can keep someone from being free who has restored or maintained the connection to their most authentic, wild self. My commitment to the animals in my care is to allow them to do just that, because, quite frankly, it's the only way to insure my own freedom as well.

Upon returning from our morning pack walk one day, weeks after Denali had recovered from her big adventure, I noticed her collar was missing. The lesson had been learned there, and I was adamant about the big dogs wearing their collars any time they were outside, so I got a replacement on her immediately. However, her regular collar (or actually, her ID tag) was special to me, and I was really irritated that it was gone. I scoured the land, but it seemed like a hopeless pursuit. Even if I narrowed it down to the ten acres where I assumed it came off, it was still like looking for a needle in a haystack.

Two weeks later, I was reflecting on everything I had been learning and all that her dognapping incident had revealed about my work. The thought came to me, I wonder if love could help me find the missing collar and tag.

Now, this was a reach, even for me. My work has made me extremely sensitive to receiving information that not too many years ago would have made me uncomfortable to consider. The first time I received a direct communication from a horse, and actually acknowledged it, I was scared to tell anyone because I didn't want to seem weird. Since that time, though, I've gotten over myself a bit, and learned to just stay open, but unattached. So I figured I'd give it a go. What would it look like to go out to the land and relate to her using the same principles that were cleaning up all my other relationships? There was no way to know without trying.

Without any clues on where to start the search, I just went out to the area where I walk with the dogs. A humility settled over me that left me feeling curious, childlike, and admittedly, a little awkward. I had never talked to the land before. With my arms soft but engaged, palms forward, at each of my sides, I internally posed the question, "Can you show me where the collar is?" Within seconds, I saw a flash in my mind, very much like a memory I didn't have, of Denali romping through a particular area of land I recognized and digging excitedly at some brush. Without taking time to judge what had just happened, I simply started moving in the direction of what I had seen, with an openness that was testing the edges of my comfort zone.

When I got to the brushy area, I thought it looked like a reasonable enough place for her to lose her collar. If she had been digging here, she easily could have gotten the collar looped on a root where it could have been tugged off as she pulled back. I just stood there in silence, refusing to entertain any of the thoughts I could hear knocking at the door to question my sanity. As I felt into my body, following the sensations from the top of my head down to my feet, which seemed no longer separate from the ground beneath them, I noticed something.

There, on the ground near my feet, was some sort of fluff, like a nest of some sort. I forgot about the collar instantly, as excitement over the prospect of potentially seeing baby wild animals entered my awareness. I very carefully and gently reached down and forward to examine the strange material. As I lifted it for closer inspection, there was Denali's missing tag, in the dirt below. The fluff was her now disintegrated collar.

Oh. My. God. It worked.

I found the needle in the freaking haystack because I had been shown the way. I had been shown the way because I stepped into an unconditionally loving relationship with the land, and she accepted my invitation to commune. What the hell?

I couldn't argue with what had just happened. I even had a witness. Before stepping out to go search, I had shared my intention, down to what I was going to experiment with. When I returned home less than 20 minutes later with the collar and a shit-eating grin, it was all the confirmation anyone would need to acknowledge it had worked.

Why did it scare me, though? Why was my first thought that I must be crazy rather than I must be made of magic? I had engaged in this dance so many times before, offering my hand to unknown possibility, just for possibility to accept, place its hand back in mine, and that still not be enough evidence to make my experience more true than my conditioning. This was going to take practice.

By my side the entire way, on most days, including that one, was Spur. He looked proud of me when I made my discovery, but he always looked proud of me, even when I sucked. That's why I needed him so much, and it's also why I needed to stop needing him. My relationship with him was the last obstacle in my path, my final dance with codependency, and I was terrified of giving it up. Many changes had been made to free him as much as I could bear, but as he approached his 12th year, I knew I was running out of time. My intuition could no longer be denied, though every trip to the vet revealed some strange reason we couldn't get a clear diagnosis. It was like the universe was trying to protect me from what I already knew. I started grieving months before the lymphoma was actually confirmed, knowing the gravity of the loss ahead, and when the news finally came, I only had two weeks left with the only soul on Earth who had ever made me feel truly seen, safe, and loved.

⊙≫⊙≪⊙

Chapter 18

RECLAMATION

So, what happens when the connection has been restored and you're now being informed by something inside more than out? Everything changes. Priorities, relationships, careers, lifestyle choices, and basically your why for everything you do is now coming from the most powerful source available: the source operating within you. I won't downplay it. In my experience, it looks and feels like total upheaval, but that's largely because I did not have an example to follow. Reclaiming the authentic self will be painful, for sure, but it doesn't have to look and feel like chaos. If you've made it this far, you already know the only thing you need to know about how to navigate the transition. Drop the story, and feel it all.

There's risk in reading this chapter if you aren't willing to drop the story. The words on these pages can easily trigger fear and anxiety about what's to come if you continue down this path. No matter how much you have to look forward to, there will be loss along the way. There is always loss in a physical existence, and that's why it is so important that we learn how to grieve like emotionally mature, wild animals. Grief need not be tied to a story. It need neither be heavy or dark or filled with sorrow. Grief is simply the physical journey between one way of operating and another when something significant changes. Reclaiming what is yours will require you to grieve.

My undomesticated animals taught me the true nature of grief. So did wild animals, but not the kind most people observe. If a wild animal can be easily observed in its natural habitat, the chances of it being untouched by domestication are unlikely at best.

We have all seen the videos circulating the internet of animals grieving like domesticated humans. I cannot begin to say how sad that makes me because the reality of it is that humans need to learn how to grieve like mature animals, and the grief that most of humanity knows is deeply mired in emotionally stunted attachment. When an emotionally mature animal experiences the pain and transition of loss, it is simply deeply felt in a wide range of physical sensations. Then it is released and the animal moves on.

When Spur died, his mother, Pippa, who had been at his side every day for all 12 years of his life, behaved quite normally throughout the entire process. There was not one noticeable difference in her in the days, weeks, or months that followed his death. The reason is because all of her needs were met, and she had never been heavily exploited to the point that she was unable to feel and process her feelings.

When one of my dearest horses died, there was an incredible response from the herd. For three days, his two closest friends stood quietly in the center of the sanctuary while the rest of the herd hung back along the most distant fence line. They stood there like this each of those days until I returned home from work. As they saw my truck approach, they moved forward to meet me while the rest of the herd fell in behind them. Three days of this and then completely back to normal—it was simply a transition. We didn't miss him. We honored him by honoring our loss and continuing on. One of the hardest lessons any of my students ever has to face is this: To miss someone is to admit we were using them for something. We don't miss those we love when we already feel whole. We just love them.

Once it is able to freely move through the body and inform it in so many ways, that love, that incredible force, is the key to reclamation. All of this work is simply about learning how to be and stay in the body, to be with and informed by sensation, and to keep the channels clear for information to be received. It's really that simple. The only thing that stands in the way is fear.

On the other side is everything you've ever imagined, and probably more. The end of suffering and the ability to access your heart's strongest desires is as simple as being able and willing to feel everything. Once you live in that place, so much of the cause of why we hurt so much more than is necessary is addressed and a lot of clarity sets in.

The clarity I'm speaking of comes with enormous gifts. One of them is immense courage. Before this work, I'd say I was generally a confident person, but there were so many areas, especially matters of the heart, where I often got myself into extremely painful situations. There were other areas I never dared venture toward out of deep insecurity. However, with my instinct, intuition, and inspiration intact, what I've found most valuable about any of this is the incredible depth of trust I now have in myself and in that which extends beyond me into the unseen. My courage, my faith, my trust has become unshakable. On top of that, I actually really like who I am today, and have healed most of the shame from my past. The transformation does not take place instantly. There are years of habitual behavioral patterns to overcome, and those all take time to correct, but the difference is that once this reclamation has occurred, it is always accessible by choice.

There are parts of myself I gave up due to trauma. The parts that loved to sing, and write, and swim got pushed to the background of surviving in a world I had not been emotionally prepared to handle. On the surface, I got by just fine, but underneath I was missing out again and again on the things I really loved, the things that brought me genuine joy.

Now, it's not that unusual for me to stop what I'm doing to go find an alpine lake I can jump into. It's not unusual for me to make time to sing or play my guitar. And it's far from unusual for me to sit down at my desk and write even though it took me nearly four decades to remember that that's what I came here to do. It sounds funny, since you're reading the second book I've written, but it wasn't until this chapter, this period of my life, that I realized I'm a writer.

When all the domestication falls away, there can be a vulnerable period of transition between who they shaped you to be and who you really are. Reclaiming the latter takes courage. You have to want more than comfort and a sense of outer security. Each step I take toward that woman I was meant to be comes with the experience of grieving each step I took away from her. It is painful but liberating, and the more I keep walking, the less pain is there, and the more easily new pain becomes to navigate.

Describing what it's like to walk in the world without fear of pain is not easy, especially when I am so aware of how uncommon that is. Pain no longer has any negative association with it in my life. It is valuable information that helps keep me moving toward, rather than away from, the things I'm here to encounter. This heightened perception does not bring unnecessary pain, or more of it than before. Instead, pain now speaks to me before it is fully present, allowing me to navigate the terrain of my existence with far more grace than I ever imagined possible.

I love animals and always will, there's no doubt about that. However, in getting back in touch with my authentic animal self, the one whose body now speaks with wild wisdom, I've realized that this was never about other animals as much as it was about understanding our attraction to them as representing our desperation to be more like them again.

My own attraction to captive, dependent animals has diminished significantly, if not entirely. That is not to say my feelings of joy or responsibility toward them has, only my desire to keep them in captivity for my own desires. I no longer need a dog to love me, because I love myself entirely. I no longer want a horse to carry me, because I've found the strength in my own power. These changes did not arise out of moral obligation; they happened because the cause of the behavior was addressed, and I found wholeness and sanctuary inside myself.

So many people are drawn to this work, these ideas, out of righteous obligation toward animals. Allow that to be your entry point, if you must, but please know now that you will, you must, walk away from such notions if you are to actually walk this path with integrity. This is about you. This is about becoming the kind of emotionally mature, wild human animal you were designed to be, because that's what our world needs in order to change, not more people thinking they know what's right and correct and true. It is time for our species to move, to speak, and to act from their inner knowing.

⊙≫⊛≪⊙

Chapter 19
INFINITE

The first day Spur didn't eat was spent lying in the cool grass at a local park. Our off-grid situation back home did not allow me to keep him very comfortable in the late summer heat, so those final days were spent driving to various locations where I knew he would find some comfort and rest. The day at the park, though, was the day I knew my time with him was coming to a close. I had brought every favorite snack of his I could think of, and he wanted none of them, so we just lay together in the grass under a huge oak tree, him on his back in my lap while I gently rocked and sang to him.

The source of the Sacramento River was another refuge in those final days. Spur could no longer move around well, so I would help him to the water's edge where his mother, Pippa, would come to his side, and we would all sit as a family in reverent silence, listening to and feeling the water flow around us. When the temperature at home had dropped enough for us to return, we'd go home and sleep, repeating the ritual the following day. I slept on the ground outside with him every night that week, staring at the beautiful fur I would soon never feel against my skin again. Allowing myself to grieve and let go, I also made sure to stay with him, fully see him, witness his pain, every step of the way.

Spur took his last breath in our vet's office. I could tell he wasn't going to leave me easily, and on his final day, when his discomfort could no longer be soothed, I made the very difficult decision to end it. I wanted so much for him to die peacefully at home, but the relationship I had formed with him made it difficult for him to let go.

He knew how much I had needed him all those years, and on his last day, I told him everything I wanted him to know about how much I loved him, how much he had taught me, how much he had inspired me, but most importantly, that even though I knew it was going to be so hard without him,

I could do it, because of him. I told him to be the brave boy I knew he was and let me learn how to stand on my own two feet. And then he was gone.

I took his body into the mountains and cleansed him in the cold run-off from an alpine lake high above us. As I wrapped him to bring him home to be with our family for the night, I saw a large stone in the creek. After placing him gently into my vehicle, I went back to the rock and picked it up. It weighed roughly the same as Spur, so I placed it in the vehicle as well, and drove them both home.

I placed his body on his bed outside so his mother and other pack mates could make their final goodbyes. Being far less domesticated than he, either situationally or through my practiced efforts, they had little to say other than a short sniff before they moved on and went back about their own business. Even his mother, who spent every single day of the last 12 years by his side, handled his transition with wild prowess and healthy detachment.

We all slept outside on the ground together that night, and the next morning, I drove Spur's body to the animal crematorium. A few days later, I drove his ashes and the rock back out to the creek where I had found it. I didn't put it back. Instead, I lowered it into my backpack, all 55 pounds of it, and then carried it up the steep 2.1-mile trail to the lake above.

The lineage of qi gong I practice is special, in that the movements are not only energy balancing and healing in and of themselves but also carry the power of archetype, each with its own spiritual and mythopoetic understanding, infusing each form with a dedicated intention through story.

I carried Spur's body, in the form of a rock, up the mountain with the qi gong form Carry Tiger to the Mountain held deeply in my consciousness. The mythology behind the form is of a Daoist master whose best friend, a tiger, had died. When the tiger died, the master gathered up his body and carried him to the top of a mountain to honor what the tiger had given to the relationship.

As I carried the "body" of my dearest dog up this mountain, I let the story of the monk and his tiger fill my awareness with parallel experience. I felt the weight of Spur's physical form on my back and the weight of grief on my heart, and each step upward, I felt that weight lighten as I gave thanks for all our beautiful, joyful memories together. By the time I reached the top, the weight felt light as a feather, and I was ready to let him go. He carried me so much farther in his short life than I had done for him in return, but I promised to carry everything he had inspired and taught me out into the world for the rest of mine.

Once I made it to the lake, I pulled the rock out and turned it into a memorial for my beloved. Then I stood in the water and offered a ceremony of nine repetitions of Carry Tiger to the Mountain. Each time my arms flowed down to gather his "body" from the earth, I scooped up a small handful of his ashes to release to the cosmos above. I then transitioned into the next form in that particular qi gong series, Phoenix Rising, and moved into nine repetitions again to balance and complete my offering. Because of all I had learned during the last few years of Spur's life, I believe I was able to fully grieve and let go of him that day. I would still have plenty of work to do in regards to letting go of guilt and shame, but my dear Spur was now free. Grieving the loss of Spur was the easy part. I was incredibly grateful that he was no longer a slave to the influence of my emotions or the codependency I had imposed on him. What came along with his death, however, was a great many other deaths I was not exactly prepared for.

When I lost him, I lost the only source of truly tried and tested unconditional love in my life. My work and seeking had taken me places that had caused an abrupt end to nearly all of my close or intimate relationships. It had isolated me at the edge of the physical wilderness. It had made me a bit of an alien to my own species. When Spur left, all of that and more became overwhelmingly apparent, and I sank into a very difficult period of healing and deep rest I now call Post-Domestication Depression.

His death was the severance of the final thread of codependency and exploitation in my life. That was worth celebrating in and of itself, but the problem was I had not matured enough to deal efficiently with what remained, which was basically every ounce of trauma that had been covered up for decades by the distraction of domestication and any other means of avoidance. I found myself on an island without a single other human who understood what I was going through. It was brutal, necessary, and ultimately led me back to myself in a way that nothing previously had been able to. It's hard to know where you're really at when you're supported by things you never thought to question, but I knew what was waiting for me in that darkness, and I chose it anyway.

The bravest thing I will ever do is choose to walk away from the subtle abuses of power I had been riding on all my life. People thought it was brave of me to give up riding horses and tell about it, but it wasn't. It just felt true and necessary. Giving up my codependency, or even facing it, took real courage. It was easier for me to talk about my transgressions against others than it was to discuss my weaknesses and insecurities born from the wounds inflicted upon me in my early development. When all the armor finally came off, it turned out I had a very scared little girl hiding inside me who had little education or modeling on what it means to be an emotionally aware and mature adult.

Fortunately, that scared little girl was only one aspect of the woman who decided to share this story with the world. There is also a fierce protector and something deeply wild and wise within me that I had only glimpsed beneath the initial layers of my own domestication. They were glimpses powerful enough to keep me on this path, for sure, but they were fleeting as a result of the quality of relationship I still chose to engage in, especially with animals, but with all sorts of other things in my life as well.

Once I was willing to give up all those externalized sources of coping, the conversation with that wild woman inside became stable and constantly accessible. Slowing down enough to change habitual patterns of thought and behavior takes time, but she's always there, waiting, when I do. Finding her, knowing her so intimately, has been the only source of courage I will ever need, and that has been worth every bit of pain along the way.

Spur showed me the kind of love I have yet to experience from another human after years of relating. He taught me the power of joy and inspiration to guide me. Denali taught me how to embody it all, and how to access the instinct and intuition that would serve me far better than any knowledge my mind could offer. I will always wish I could have helped Spur achieve the level of wild that Denali has always known, but I suppose he didn't need my help. He is certainly wild now, after all, and he continues to guide me without the interference of his conditioning—or his short stubby legs.

A few weeks after his death, I was gifted with a beautiful hand-blown glass hummingbird, infused with the remainder of Spur's ashes. Hummingbirds are often how I receive his message to follow joy, and it no longer surprises me to look up and find a hummer nearby when I'm thinking of him.

On my first trip with the pack to a remote mountain lake after he was gone, I found myself standing in the water, wishing so much that he could be there with us, and when I looked down, there was a small metal hummingbird in the mud at my feet. It didn't even seem weird. I just laughed and picked it up so he could join us. Now, the glass hummingbird that carries his ashes hangs above the corner of my desk, letting me know when I need a little help. Don't ask me how, but on the days I get stuck emotionally, the glass hummer faces the wall, turned away from me. When I'm in the flow of life, it faces me directly. He's looking right at me this moment. As it turns out, in death, Spur has learned how to move in response to me the way Denali does here with paws on the ground.

As I write these words, nearing the end of what I came here to say, I feel unable to fully express the extent of what has occurred within and around me. It may simply be too soon to put it all into words, but I believe the foundational principles too important to withhold until I can speak to it more eloquently. I suppose, at the end of the day, what I would most want you to know is this. You deserve to walk humbly upon Earth, with grace bestowed by the magnificent power of life itself. Domestication, both your own and that imposed on others, will have you seeking salvation forever. Only when we become wild again do we remember we are infinite.

Chapter 20
THE WILD UNKNOWN

Knowing is a convenient coping mechanism for those with the intellectual capacity to think they actually know. Believing we know how things should be or how to make them so, provides a false element of control over our lives. It makes us feel safe in a world where staying a step ahead seems to be the thing to strive for.

What scares people the most about the wild is just how little knowing exists within the context of what it means to be wild. It is not as if the wild ones do not acquire useful knowledge through experience, but what they lack is the attachment to using that knowledge to bypass the greater body of wisdom that is constantly accessible through their present, feeling reality. The only thing that is truly known in the wild is embodied in the now. Trusting in that wild now is the access point to all greater wisdom.

The greatest teachers and mentors to ever cross my path had one singular thing in common: They all had a deeply intimate relationship with the unseen world, exemplified in a way that left no room to question their faith in a power greater than their limited concept of self. They exhibited sacrament.

It is alluring enough to observe this quality in animals, but to stumble upon a human who is consciously choosing to trust in something so powerfully unknown, so completely opposed to their own conditioning, is a catalyzing experience for even the most domesticated among us. Religion cannot offer this to people, as most of its followers are simply giving their power away to something they have chosen to believe. No, what I am speaking to here is a direct relationship with the source of truth that most religions are born from; an actual ongoing conversation with Creator, as individuated creators ourselves.

As I take each new, humble step into my own alignment with the wildest and wisest version of myself, I know only two things: I have no idea what lies ahead, and I know I can trust myself completely to navigate the wilderness of my life. That may not seem like much, but to someone who has suffered and overcome enormous struggle throughout what has been an often painful life, it is everything. Now, there is nothing outside myself I give more attention to than my own inner landscape. Every day, I am listening, questioning, recalibrating. In service to that, I am compassionate toward myself, and have learned how to recognize the difference between my trauma and the authentic me I can turn to at any time for love and support.

It takes immense courage to live in the unknown before one has learned how to feel the full extent of their feelings and be in right relationship to emotion. People resist giving up control only until they learn how to stay in an embodied relationship to fear. Once that is achieved, courage is more conceptual than experience.

I've often been told how brave I am. I wouldn't say that about myself. It doesn't require bravery to do the things I do. I'm simply in right relationship to pain and my feeling animal body. I want to experience and be informed by all of it. I love being a human animal, and those who don't are those who have yet to learn what that means. Far too often the phrase "I'm only human" is used to describe some inadequacy with our species, when the truth about what we are could not be farther from such ignorance.

To be human is the most incredible opportunity imaginable. To be a fully connected, intrinsically guided animal who also has the self-awareness and intellectual capacity to deliberately create from an expanded awareness is not something to be ashamed of – to the contrary. The error is not in our humanity but in our domestication. Our perpetuation of domestication in our relationships keeps us cyclically stuck in the error.

This book took years to write because for a long time I did not actually understand what it was about, and I surely did not embody its message. The idea originally centered around the most loving way to relate to animals and all the harm caused by domestication, and while that's still relevant and addressed here, that is not why you are reading these words.

You are reading this book because something in you desperately longs to be free, and something inside you has stirred enough to believe that an answer might be found in these pages. I am deeply sorry to say you won't find many answers here, only maybe a lantern lighting the way. The only answer you need has been within you this entire time, but not in the form of a concept or thought. Your body simply needs you to stay present with it long enough to learn the full extent of its feeling potential. That's all that is required to know everything you will ever need to know, but it requires an unwavering faith in your innate ability to navigate a wildly unfolding unknown.

There were no humans to guide me or teach me the entirety of this process. There were plenty of teachers speaking to relevant things, but no one was addressing the dependence upon the unearned privilege of external forms of emotional regulation, especially that which is provided by riding on the power of captive, dependent animals. It is one thing to "do the work" when you can reach for the dog for comfort or climb on the back of a horse to support your process; it is another thing entirely to pressure-test the work of healing without abusing power to do so.

When nothing is known, everything becomes possible. The last ten years of my life have been dedicated to serving the animals in my care and the people who want to learn about this. There has not been room for much else, because choosing this path has literally cost me everything.

As many often do that are bringing a novel concept to light, I became overly identified with "my" work, which is not mine at all, and merely the practical application of authentic love. My take on it, especially in the particular way it is done with captive, dependent animals may be my own creation, but we've had plenty of resources teaching us about love for centuries. We just weren't willing to question the one relationship that could reveal it all, because the very traumatic nature of our own domestication does not prepare us to do so.

Ten years ago, through our mutual admiration of horses, I met a woman who stopped me dead in my tracks the first time our eyes met. In that moment, I recognized her in a way that I will likely never be able to explain. I loved her completely and instantaneously, and in her allowing of that, we formed an unconditional thread that has kept us bonded through many forms of connection, despite periods of time and space apart. It was my love for this woman that inspired this work and made it possible for me to see what my stallion, Shai, was reflecting the day I finally learned how to love unconditionally, drop into my body, and let my heart break.

I feel so fortunate to have stumbled across a mirror in this life that remains an endless well of wisdom to return to. And we all have that. What do you love so much that it breaks your heart? Let it be your muse. Do not ever try to tame or claim it, less you desire to get enormously distracted from your path. Honor it with the deepest respect, as your beloved, and let that inspiration carry you into your destiny, even if it moves you away from the very thing that made you come alive. What you'll find if you truly commit is that the muse was inside of you all along, and wild hearts can't be broken. The animals showed me the way when I eliminated all the obstacles to listening. When I finally understood, what I found was not solace in another being but sanctuary in myself. I could never be safe for another without first being my own safe home.

Applying Sanctuary13 to my relationships with other humans, situations, and especially myself, took a bit more work than with the animals. That's not to say at all that I have mastered it, because I definitely have not. What I have mastered is my ability to notice when I'm out of alignment with what my body knows is true. I don't always know what to do with that awareness, but I know how to surrender to it.

It does not matter who or what shows up in front of me, there is a center I can always return to, and that is the most powerful transformation of my life. I do not desire to live in a present state of awareness at all times. I desire to be able to choose one, to retain some access to it, at any time, and that I have achieved.

My integrity with and embodiment of this work came through one key change in my life. I stopped living for others, including the animals, and began making my relationship to my own soul the number one priority and relationship in my life, trusting that if I did so, everything else would fall into place. That, by far, is the most courageous move I have ever made. Because I know that I will never again abandon myself, I am able to trust my own body's discernment over any outside influence or authority. The power in that experience is ineffable. What I can tell you is, for the very first time, I really love, trust, and accept who and what I am. There is a safety in that which fosters great courage and is palpable to everyone who comes into contact with it. The power of that influence is far greater, and far more trustworthy, than any I previously had with words or confidence alone.

To paraphrase the famous words of poet Mary Oliver: We do not have to be good. All we must do is allow the soft animal of our body to love what it loves. The love she is speaking to there is the kind only the body knows. What softens your resistance? What brings out your most authentic, enthusiastic YES?

As it turns out, I do not love being weighed down by responsibility and obligation, with no time or resources to enjoy the things I do love. I love swimming in alpine lakes that chill me to the bone. I love savoring a carefully crafted cup of coffee. I love to sing. I love going on epic adventures in the wilderness and running through the forest with my pack. I love to let my body move the way it wants to move, have intimate conversations, be touched, make love, and serve with a whole heart. Apparently, I love to write. It is in the trusting of our Yes that we find the courage to brave the unknown, and the joy in honoring what we love is what makes the difficulty of undomesticating our lives worth every step.

I do not know what lies ahead, and I am thrilled about that. It means everything is waiting for me, everything. I just have to keep moving toward what my body says Yes to and away from anything that feels like an insult to my soul. Being wild involves understanding how to do so with grace and discernment, backed by the wisdom of clear instinct, intuition, and inspiration.

The animals in my care, and the ones I have had the pleasure of knowing in the wilderness, have taught me more in ten years than what centuries of domesticated humanity has had to offer. No more will I be informed through the lens of domestication. Denali may have taught me how to run with wolves, but now, in this animal body as conduit for my soul's instruction, I run as one.

⊙>>>⊘<<<⊙

Denali and Spur

AFTERWORD

Ren has delivered us into a world of consideration, a world that moves us beyond connection toward an authentic potentiality of communion with all our relations, primarily beginning with ourselves. Her writing is at once new but also ancient, in the capacity humans have always had to move with the forces of nature, to be moved by them, to be deeply informed by them versus to attempt to command them.

This book is a call and response—a call to rework how we have positioned ourselves as a species, and where we hold ourselves on the continuum of all of life.

There is much to throw up our hands with in regards to the devastation our species has brought to this planet, and as a result, a field of complacency and an equal, oppositional state of rage. These are the current polarizations of our times.

Ren offers a soulful response, in a world that is desperately hungry not only for a compassionate trajectory but also for a true recognition of self-responsibility. Sanctuary13 is a way to look at, examine, and reconfigure our interactions and our intentions with all beings. This soulful reverence provides a window to the reality of how our relations, in fact, weave us. How, or if, we evolve, not as a species that dominates, but as a species that participates in harmony and in the actualization of civility, is the question we must contend with.

The same underlying question presents itself through my own work at Breath.Body.Touch. Ren and I have influenced one another's passionate way of bringing ourselves and our work into the world since our first meeting in 2016. True friendship challenges, embraces, and invokes a deep growth, and we have catalyzed one another's direction in a beautiful way.

Each element of Sanctuary13 is crucial in this process because the system is a reflection of our inner complexity and wholeness. Nothing—body, mind, psyche, trauma, soul, nor emotion—may be left out of a human being's reach toward freedom. The application of these principles can be utilized toward work with animals, humans, one's relationship to anything, because it is ultimately rooted in reorienting toward self. Once we recover our origins, there is no limitation for the potential of our existence. Practice is the grindstone and these pages the jumping-off point toward reclaiming the inner wild sanctuary of soul.

To fall in love with the unseen,

invisible energies of this world

is to begin a path of liberation and freedom

To become both the wild and the wilderness

To pierce through the veil that our conscious and unconscious patterns

of domesticity bears on the soul

To become a safe harbor for the manifestation

of the true energies of your unique destiny

We are not just pitched but designed

for this soulful reckoning

and the passage it affords.

—**Jaye Marolla**
Thai Bodywork practitioner and
Qigong, Yoga and Martial Arts instructor
www.breathbodytouch.com

ABOUT THE AUTHOR

Photo by Brandy Setzer

Ren Hurst is an author, mentor, tracker, and guide helping people navigate the wilderness of their inner lives and relationships and restoring connection to their most authentic, emotionally mature, wild, human animal nature.

A former professional horsewoman, Ren has reverse-engineered the dynamics of animal training to produce a body of work called Sanctuary13. This work is now available and offered through the nonprofit Wild Wisdom, Inc., as part of their mission to address the trauma of domestication.

You can connect with Ren at **Instagram.com/rendermewild**
or visit her website at **www.rendermewild.com**

To support Wild Wisdom, Inc., and access more Sanctuary13,
please visit **www.undomesticate.me**

FINDHORN PRESS

Life-Changing Books

Learn more about us and our books at
www.findhornpress.com

For information on the Findhorn Foundation:
www.findhorn.org